Balancing
My
SeeSaw

Through
Life's
Ups
and
Downs

JustSue

THANKS, EVERYBODY!!

There are so many people I would like to thank, but I'm only going to mention a few:

First and foremost, I thank *Jesus Christ*. He has been with me through all of my pains and pleasures, my ups and my downs.

Next, I owe GREAT gratitude to my editor and friend, *Sue Scott*. Without her, this book might never have been written. She helped me to put all my thoughts into a playground theme.

I also lift up the counselors I have been with during some very difficult seasons of my life: *Shelly Chenevert, Sheree Harrington* and last but not least, *Karen Gemboski.*

And thank you to *all of my family and friends* who have been on the various rough rides with me on the Playground of Life and who have still loved me through it all.

"My message is not my own, it comes from God who sent me." ~ John 7:16 (NLT)

Contents

Message from the Author: vi

We All Have a Story x

Voice of the Shepherd...................................xi

Soon You Will See xiii

PLAYGROUND BULLIES

CHAPTER 1: Picking Sides 1

It's So Gray 5

Sticks & Stones.. 7

CHAPTER 2: Round & Round She Goes...21

See No Evil..22

What Goes Around, Comes Around 28

Tug of War..35

Infidelity..36

From: Black & Blue To: You 39

READY? HERE WE GO!

CHAPTER 3: Hold on Tight 45

Moving Forward...51

Wide Awake...54

Significant 58

Restore 66

CHAPTER 4: Following the Leader 69

Disillusioned 72

God Bless this Mess 81

Standing by My Convictions 89

CHAPTER 5: Tagged… But Not Out 93

Amplified! 95

Why Can't I? 97

S.T.O.P. 98

Turn on the Quiet 103

I Promise You Friend 114

SWINGING FOR THE FENCES

CHAPTER 6: Up the Downside 119

CHAPTER 7: Who Wants to Play? 147

On the Playground of Life 160

CHAPTER 8: Ready or Not 173

Evidence of Spring 173

Be Someone New 180

Easy as ABC 183

More From the Author: 189

Message from the Author:

You may notice that throughout this book, I purposely capitalized the letter "S" in the word "seesaw" when referring to how life can feel for me. It helps depict the ups and downs that life inevitably brings. My own SeeSaw began when I was a stay-at-home mother of three children, all very close in age. I was extremely busy and found it very difficult to spend quality time with the Lord in prayer. Whenever I did try, I would fall asleep out of exhaustion. I would also be so tired that I would fall asleep as I read stories to my children when tucking them into bed at night. I would suddenly hear "Mom! Mom!" as they tried to wake me so they could hear the rest of their story.

One day, I was speaking to a friend who suggested that I pray to God as I go through my day. Pray as I wash the dishes, pray as I fold the laundry — invite the Lord into my crazy busy world of being a mother. He could see me and He understood what I was going through during that phase of my life. Those prayers turned into conversations with Him, and I have never stopped that practice. I am in constant contact with the Lord.

Since I carry on a conversation with God all throughout my day, I thought it would be really interesting to let you into my world of conversations with Him. Then you can see how He is always there on the SeeSaw with me and how He helps me to be balanced. Are you in need of finding stability? Let's explore the "playground" together.

As the Lord has been in the process of showing me things that He wants to work on with me, it hasn't all been a walk in the park. There have been times when I went through some trials. But He showed me a passage in Romans that I have leaned on for many, many years. It has brought me such encouragement. Romans 8:28 says: *And we know that all things work together for good to those who love God, to those who are the called according to His purpose.* Whenever He works all things together for me, I say God did an "8:28." It is my prayer that you will be able to see God's 8:28's in your life, and that it brings some type of healing for you — healing that only comes through Jesus, with our cooperation. Yes, we have a part to do too. Even if it is just simply having faith. Having enough faith can bring about miraculous results! Trust me, friend, you will learn this as you read on.

Despite some traumatic experiences I've been through, I want you to see just how faithful God can be. No matter how high or low the SeeSaw goes, the Lord never gets off of it and does not leave me alone to fight the battles I encounter. He is always right there, helping and encouraging me.

It has been my hope that my experiences can somehow be an inspiration for you as you face your own life's ups and downs, and that what I share will bring a sense of balance and blessing to you and your SeeSaw.

"For Your kingdom is an everlasting kingdom. You rule throughout all generations. The LORD always keeps His promises; He is gracious in all He does ... the battle is not yours, but God's ... you will not need to fight in this battle ... stand still and see the Salvation of the Lord." [1]

---

[1] Psalm 145:13 (NLT), 2 Chronicles 20:15,17

We All Have a Story

We are all on a journey full of little events that add up to our own unique story. No one has the same one. When our stories are shared though, common ground can be discovered. This will help to make us aware that we're not the only ones going through these experiences. I believe God will use this book to help and encourage you with your own life story.

In 1993, I wrote a poem titled, "Voice of the Shepherd." I would like to share it with you. Some people claim to have a life *verse*. Well, this is my life *poem*. It has been the catalyst to my life *story* that I am living out each day.

[Just a suggestion: It is best if you can find someone to read it to you while your eyes are closed. Sometimes we need to close our eyes in order to see and hear things more clearly. I know it doesn't make sense, but trust me, it works.]

Voice of the Shepherd

Shhh! Do you hear Me?... Close your eyes,
and you will hear Me.
Shhh! Do you see Me?... Look inside,
and you will see Me.
Shhh! Do you feel Me?... Be still,
and you will feel Me.

I'm in your heart, just waiting to be found.
Turn off the TV. Turn off the radio.
Turn off the useless talk.
I need to be heard… you need to hear Me.

Then you will find love.
Then you will find peace.
Then you will find true happiness & joy.

Fear not... for you have been
called by name.
Listen to the story — made just for you.

Shhh! Stop and hear your story.
Shhh! Be still, and feel your story.
Arise! Then *live* your story.

Fear not, for I am with you always...
Listen to the Voice of The Shepherd.

"Ask and it will be given to you; seek and you will find; knock, and it will be opened to you. For everyone who asks receives, and he who seeks finds, and to him who knocks it will be opened."
~ *Matthew 7:7-8*

I want you to know that it is *His* voice you are reading, not just mine. It all comes from Him, by the Holy Spirit working through my pen and/or my typing fingers. My writing, when I step out of the way, comes from His Spirit, and brings life to my words.

This book is written because I am hoping that my life experiences can somehow be an inspiration for you, or someone you know who is experiencing extreme ups and downs in life. I think I have finally learned some good coping skills that work for me and maybe they will for you as well. My faith in the Good Shepherd has helped me to navigate through my life's ups and downs.

There were times that I was on the playground as the sun began to set, and I suddenly found myself in the dead of night. Knowing that He will lead me safely Home, has helped me go through some of the scariest times of my life. Even though I couldn't see or feel Him, I know He carried me through those darkest of times.

Soon You Will See

What can you do on a bright shining day?
Stay close to Me, and I'll show you
The Way.

I know how much you hate those dark, dreary
days. There's hope for the future,
you'll see the sun's rays.

Soon the light will come straight from
My Son. He's up here in Heaven,
He's the true Holy One.

At the same time, He can be deep
within you. It's all a mystery,
but it really is true.

To be together forever with Me,
it won't take money; My Son paid the fee.
Listen real closely, I'm calling you now.
Ask a believer and they'll show you how.

My Son came to you there, a long time ago.
Soon He'll be back — Say "yes,"
don't say "no."

So down on your knees, say
"God, You're the One."
It's true, then you'll become
My daughter or son.

What can you do come rain or come shine?
Stay close to Me, and know that you're Mine.

*"Show me Your ways, O LORD, teach me Your
paths. Lead me in Your truth and teach me, for You
are the God of my salvation. On You I wait
all the day." ~ Psalm 25:4-5*

PLAYGROUND BULLIES

CHAPTER 1:

Picking Sides

I have this horrible habit: I choose to learn things the hard way. I am praying that if you are able to identify with any of my experiences, you will be able to make better choices, in order to alleviate as much pain as possible. Yet I have to admit it was not easy sharing this with you. I struggled a lot trying to write on the subject of an unhealthy marriage that led to a divorce. I came across my journal from that chapter of my life. As I read it, I found myself going through the same negative feelings that I had gone through all those years ago.

As I began writing this book based on those journal entries, I became bitter all over again. I noticed myself trying to prove how *I* was mistreated, and how wrong *he* was. I didn't like what I wrote and even changed the wording of a poem that sounded too self-righteous. I recognized that I still had not fully forgiven him. I thought I did years ago. I found that it was unhealthy for me to not only stir up my tragic past word for word, but I feared that you, my reader, would find yourself being poisoned by my words instead of helped.

For your sake as well as my sake, I made the hard choice to release all the resentment and anger I was feeling. I asked Jesus to take it from me and heal my damaged emotions. By forgiving the people who hurt me and giving them back to God to deal with, I was able to share the following pages of a very turbulent time, without the unforgiveness sneaking into the story. I wanted you to hear about the faithfulness of God and the lessons I learned through it all, while helping you understand the pain, but not focusing on it. I had to remember:

"…the battle is not yours, but God's … you will not need to fight in this battle … stand still and see the salvation of the LORD." ~ 2 Chronicles 20:15, 17

I still find it necessary to tell you about my errors and some dark times in order for you to see God's grace and how He brought me out better on the other side, but by "standing still" and trusting in God to fight the battle, I can write about them without reliving all the pain of the abuse.

While going through the process of getting a divorce, I found myself writing some very personal accounts that I didn't think would be read by anyone else. It helped me to work through all of my emotions, especially trying to pinpoint the emotional abuse I was going through. I wrote a number of poems as well. God has healed me enough that I am now able to share some of them with you in this book. I hope they will speak to you if you are going through an abusive situation in your life. Let me start by giving you an idea of how abusive relationships can begin, or at least how one of mine did:

It was 5:00 AM, and I couldn't sleep. So, I got out of bed and went to the local coffee shop where I wrestled once again, with some very important questions: Should I get married again? Should it be to this man? The marriage to my children's father didn't last. What makes me think this one will be different? But I don't want to be lonely and alone, and besides two paychecks will be better than one.

I should have paid attention to all the red flags, but out of fear I chose to ignore them. When we married, I found out he wasn't as wealthy as I thought. All the money he spent on me while we were dating had been put on credit cards. He then took our wedding gift money to pay them off. The financial security I had hoped for was only a facade. Ignoring red flags has its consequences.

After five or six years, I began leaving him and then returning back to him... over and over again. *Afterall, I was a Christian and Christians don't get divorced,* I told myself. I hoped that if I prayed enough, things would get better. But they did not. I tried my best to stay in the unhealthy marriage. But after seven years, I eventually left him for the final time…

*****

I paused from writing for a minute to go feed my cat, and when I did, the Lord led me to open up a book on my kitchen table. It is titled: "Think, Act, Be Like Jesus," by Randy Frazee with Robert Noland. On page 10, I read: "God wants to work *through* us, but first He must work *on* us. A deeper work takes place in the individual for the greater work to go out to the world … The Christian life is about who you are becoming for the sake of others." Those words made me realize that it is what God has done *in* me through these trials that has given me the strength and victory to share the rest of my story with you.

It's So Gray…

I remember crying out to God one night: Father, I really need Your help! I feel like I am going insane. That man I married said to me: "I have never hit you!" Doesn't he remember all those times he "hit" me with his words of anger? His words of anger and the subtle, underhanded comments he makes, make me feel beat-up and unsure of myself — causing me to question my own judgments; especially when I do as I have been told, only to be told later on that I am wrong again. That then leads to more of his anger, more put-downs, and more confusion.

But this can't be an abusive marriage, can it? We're both Christians who go to church, so this can't be an abusive marriage... right? If I just pray a little more, and try to please him, then we'll be okay... God, am I wrong? Something just isn't right with us, but I can't put my finger on it, because it's not black and it's not white, it's so... *gray!*

My daughter, you aren't imagining things. The truth is he is damaging you by slinging hateful and hurtful words at you. But the good news is My grace can be found at any time, and any place. And *that* can never be taken away from you!

Stay with Me and you'll be fine. Hold

onto My words of encouragement — words that build you up, not tear you down. You are a beautiful person whom I love very much, and I don't like the way he's treating you. No one should be treated that way.

Sticks & Stones

They say names don't hurt,
but what do they know?
They cause so much pain and
resentments to grow.

Life is too short; it's gone in an instant.
Don't stay in the abuse;
it's all right to be distant.

There are times when it's best
for you *not* to stay.
When they tell you "Get home,"
just say, "There's no way!"

Speak kindly to all; uplift one another.
'Cause after all, we're "sister & brother."
God pays attention to all of us here.
He adores and upholds us; to Him we are dear.

Self-esteem is a problem; we *can* get it back. With Christ at our center, He'll put us on track.

> *"But in that coming day no weapon turned against you will succeed. You will silence every voice raised up to accuse you. These benefits are enjoyed by the servants of the LORD, their vindication will come from me. I, the LORD have spoken."*
>
> ~ Isaiah 54:17 (NLT)

It was the fall of 2009 and I had left him for the final time. I had left him on other occasions, only to feel bad for him and then return. I was also told by well-meaning people that leaving wasn't the "Christian thing to do." I finally knew the truth, and I had put to bed that lie. I had had enough!

When I left, I had no idea how I was going to survive on my own. I would be living on a limited income, and it wouldn't be enough to rent an apartment. Instead, I rented a storage space for most of my belongings. Then, I ended up at my Grampa's house with my mother who was living there at the time. My Grampa was in a nursing facility, but he was more than happy to let me live there. My mother and I each had our own routines and habits, but we managed to get along just fine.

The following pages are based on entries I had written in my journal as I was going through the process of the divorce. I've put them here in hopes that by sharing this journey with you, you will see that with God's help, the ups and downs of divorce can eventually make you stronger:

> While doing my 12-Step Inventory with my Celebrate Recovery[2] sponsor, I found out I am not the only Christian to be going through this. It has been said that not everything that is faced can be changed, but nothing can be changed until it is faced.[3] Tonight, I'm just concentrating on breathing. I've been forgetting to do that. I have been holding it in.

---

[2] Celebrate Recovery is a faith-based 12-Step Program where Jesus is our Higher Power.

[3] James Baldwin, *The New York Times Book Review*, 1962

Lord, how come I draw closer to You, hear Your Holy Spirit more clearly, and Scripture really speaks to me, whenever I leave that man?

~~~

I am starting to feel bad for him and the fact that he is now alone. Oh, wait. Last time I left, he ordered cable, bought a van, and spent money like there was no tomorrow. I really shouldn't feel bad for him.

~~~

God, help me discern what is true.
Do you want us to remain together?
I am so confused.

~~~

I got out of bed because I couldn't stand being there any longer with the bad thoughts and dreams. And also, because I didn't want to worry my mother.

~~~

The tight knot in my stomach is lessening.
I don't fully know yet why, but it is.

~~~

Peace like a river, despite being separated from him. Got out of bed this morning. Why? God, of course — I couldn't do it on my own. I went to the Celebrate Recovery meeting and received continued peace. It was God's gift to me.

~~~

Getting out of bed was easier today. I received a book on forgiveness from my mother's friend.

~~~

I took a literal step forward and went for a walk. If someone from my 12-Step Group hadn't called needing a ride, I probably would not have gone to the group. I'm so glad I did, because I took another step and opened up at the group with the other women there. I want to be open and honest before God. After the group I went to the bookstore. I got down on one knee, as if looking at the lower shelves of CD's, and made a commitment to God that I would do whatever He wanted me to do.

While driving I felt peace and not fear.

~~~

I feel convicted that I am doing the right
thing. I realized that I am right where God
wants me to be. I am content with myself —
no more nightmares; no more self-doubts;
no more depression; no more trying
to please him.

~~~

I am thankful that a decision has been made.
Our marriage is over. It saddens me, but
now we are no longer living "in limbo." We
now know what we are doing: we're going
separate ways. I'm also grateful that I no
longer fear him. After finishing my inventory
with my Celebrate Recovery sponsor I felt so
free! My burdens had been lifted.

~~~

I met with my counselor today. She helped
me to realize that I am not unbalanced.
It was because of all the up-and-down
swings I went through in the marriage.
He always had me guessing things and he
made me fear my own sanity. I was so

unsure of myself. I no longer fear everything, like I had been doing in the past.

My counselor also described me as being at the edge of a cliff and too afraid to jump over to the next one. But now I have been able to do it. I know it's because I let go and let Christ bridge the gap from the old into the new. Praise God! I pictured two cliffs with a gap between them and then pictured the cross of Jesus lining up between them so I would be able to walk across on the gift of His cross to the other side.

~~~

I went to the bank to remove my name from the joint checking account. They wouldn't let me; he has to do it! I can't understand that. It was really discriminating; he could do whatever he wanted with the accounts, but I wasn't allowed to. It feels so unfair!

When he called yesterday, he said in his message, "Call me back, if you choose to." Well, I CHOOSE NOT TO.

I changed my address at the post office

and packed almost everything from the house while he was at work. God, this is so hard. Why did it come to this? This feels right, but it still stinks. I have been so busy, trying to be strong and upbeat about moving out. But I finally was able to cry about it tonight, which I hadn't done, since leaving him.

~~~

He invited me to dinner, and I told him I couldn't go. I have Celebrate Recovery to go to (and besides, I didn't want to go with him.) The Lord helped me to see how unhealthy it would be for me to go.

~~~

IT'S A MIRACLE! When I was with him, I couldn't wait to go to sleep at night and I struggled tremendously to get up the next day. Sometimes I slept twelve hours straight, in order to escape. Right now, it's 11:00 PM and I'll be getting up at 6:30 AM tomorrow.

Praise God! Hallelujah! I don't want to go to bed at night, and I want to get up in the morning!

~~~

He texted me today, saying he would be praying for me to have peace today. I didn't respond. I wrote poems about what I am going through. It was very helpful. God, you know that I do not wish to be bitter through this divorce. I just want to be thankful it's over, and to move on in service to You — my only Strength and my only Provider.

~~~

Parts of today were difficult. I miss having someone to share my life with. But I have to keep reminding myself about the SeeSaw pattern that has continued, especially over the last year or two: Things get bad at home … I leave … I feel sorry for him … he makes promises … I return … things are fine for a while … things get bad again — and so the cycle goes.

~~~

God, last night I had a dream that I had gone back to him. I could hear my thoughts: Oh no, what have I done? I shouldn't be here! This isn't right! How do I go back to my family again? They'll most likely turn me away this time. I've burned that bridge.

Strangely, I also experienced that sick feeling in my stomach, telling me that I had done something terribly wrong. I could actually feel it, even though I was dreaming. I was so thankful that I had that dream. Was that from You? Did You give it to me so I would make sure not to go back to him again?

Yes, it was Me. I speak to you through the dreams you have while your body is sleeping. Sometimes it is the only way to help you sort things out that you're not able to do while you're awake. I'm glad you remembered how it made you feel, because it really wouldn't have been wise for you to go back again, and I wanted to make sure that you knew that.

~~~

Yahoo! Today is National Face Your Fear Day. I found this out tonight, after I faced my fear and conquered it. He called my mom and asked her how I was. Later he called and left me a message to call him.

After praying with my Celebrate Recovery sponsor, I was ready. I braced myself for the head games I knew he would be using against me. I held onto God's strong hand and called him: He wanted to know how I could face God after breaking my vow. He wanted to know where we stood and if I would be showing up like the previous time that I left him and hung signs on trees saying that I was sorry, in hopes that he would take me back. [He had convinced me it was all my fault.]

He didn't want to be wasting his time texting me or attending support groups for family members of the mentally ill if I was planning on divorcing him. He couldn't see any justification or legal reason before God, but he will go along if I file.

"You have no reason to leave. I never hit you or cheated on you!" he said.

I told him, "I know in my heart that I am justified before God, and I don't need to justify myself to you or to anyone else."

I didn't yell; I just calmly stated my point, to which he had no reply. He will be changing the locks this weekend, which means I'll need to call ahead of time for him to open the door.

As Martin Luther King, Jr. said: "Free at last, free at last. Thank God Almighty we're free at last!" Thank You, Jesus! Now I know what my purpose is. It's to help others who are suffering from the "Gray Zone" of emotional abuse.

It can be very difficult to look up when you have been knocked down every time you begin to rise. But remember, *God upholds all who fall and raises up all who are bowed down.*[4] God says:

Be bold, rise up, move on; you can do this with My power! Picture Me, your Father, tenderly placing My hands on your cheeks and lifting your head, as I remind you of who you really are — someone I created and for whom I have such an endearing

---

[4] See Psalm 145:14

love. I was willing to send My Son to earth for you to remind you of that. Take the time to immerse yourself in My Word, you will find comfort. I have put into words My plans for you, as My children.

Thank You for Your Word, Lord! It does bring me such comfort! So much comfort that when I hold Your Bible up to my chest and hug it tight, it feels like we are actually hugging together.

I see your tears when no one is there to comfort you. [5] That may be how you feel, but I am the great Comforter, the Holy Spirit. I will guide you and protect you, for I am your Shepherd.

At times you felt you were in prison, and lonely, even though you were surrounded by people. As you know, the prison you find yourself in can become strangely comfortable, your imaginable safety zone. You no longer allow visitors, because you're afraid of being hurt again; like a

---

[5] See Ecclesiastes 4:1

turtle retreating into your shell, you feel helpless and powerless. All that is going to change. You will no longer be a victim; you will become victorious.

You need to realize that I am already *in* the prison with you, encouraging you, so allow Me to *free you*, to unlock the door into the freedom of the life I have planned for you. I'm here when you are ready to begin your new life. Just say the word.

CHAPTER 2:
Round & Round She Goes

Do you remember those playground spinners? We used to call them merry-go-rounds, but they weren't very merry; there were no pretty painted-ponies or gentle ups and downs. They just spun around as fast as whoever was pushing them could make them go. And if whoever was pushing them was not kind or considerate, what started out to be fun could become a dizzying nightmare. If we tried to get off, we might just get flung clear across the park. So, we'd hang on for dear life until it slowed down and promise ourselves that we wouldn't ever get on one of those again… until the next time.

If you haven't been in an abusive relationship, you may find yourself wondering *why doesn't she just leave him?* Let me share with you how things can look when you find yourself stuck in a "playground spinner" of a marriage, hanging on just holding your breath, with a bully pushing you.

See No Evil…

"Let your eyes look straight ahead, and your eyelids look right before you. Ponder the path of your feet, and let all your ways be established. Do not turn to the right or the left; remove your foot from evil." ~ Proverbs 4:25-27

I remember when my children were young, their minds were like little tape recorders. They would watch a movie and then would quote the exact words that were used in the movie as if they had seen it a hundred times.

A lot of times we can get a song stuck in our head. We hear it playing over and over again.

22

There's something that happens in our minds when we see or hear things. It can be very difficult to erase the memory of them. And because of that, we need to be careful of what we allow in there. That unwanted "tape recording" can spin around our head for a very long time.

One day my husband brought the disease of pornography into our home... and into our bedroom. I call it a disease because it is progressive and can lead to death — death of the soul and mind — if not caught in time. Very slowly and methodically I was trapped into a net of pornography. In the end, it was one of the things that contributed to destroying and killing our marriage. It all started out as something so simple as him reading me a story. Then the stories changed to X-rated. I don't ever want to hear anything like that again. They are called dirty stories and dirty magazines for a reason — they leave an unforgettable stain.

Bringing those words and images into my mind caused me to hear and see them over and over again too. It was something that I tried to

23

keep hidden, and I didn't want anyone to know what I had been involved in. What I tried so hard to hide from others, was eating away at me. I didn't speak up and say to him that it was not good to be reading these stories. The biggest reason is because pornography can numb and kill our soul. Pornography attacks our senses through hearing and seeing and invades our thoughts. It gives us an unrealistic and degrading view of what love really is.

One night my husband asked me to come watch something on the computer. When I saw what was on there, it totally disgusted me. I had absolutely no desire to watch; if I were to, not only would I have *seen* the evil, but I would also have been haunted by the memory of *hearing* the sounds in my mind as well. I finally spoke up and said, "That's it! I've had enough!" I drew the line in the sand. I would not go down that dirty road anymore!

> "It is better to be persecuted for having said the truth, than to be favored for having flattered." ~ *Augustine*

I started to see more clearly that for my husband this was an addiction, spinning out of control. As much as I was ready to quit cold turkey, I needed to understand why pornography was so addicting. I knew that biological reactions are experienced in the middle of any addiction, so I looked up some words in the Merriam Webster dictionary. Here are the paraphrased definitions:

> **En-dor'-phin** – noun – Any of a group of hormones *secreted* within the brain and nervous system and having a number of physiological functions. They activate the body's *opiate* receptors, causing an *analgesic* effect similar to morphine.

> **An-al-ge'-sic** – noun – An agent producing diminished sensation to pain without loss of consciousness.

It's the chemicals like adrenalin and endorphins released in our brains, that we get addicted to because they trigger our pleasure center and override emotional and/or physical pain. Those chemicals are what tend to make whatever we're experiencing stick in our memories, whether what's happen is ecstatic or traumatic.

I, personally, am already super sensitive to sights and sounds. While I was in high school, a teacher pointed out how subliminal messages can be used in advertising to create the release of endorphins in us, without us even realizing that it is happening. He showed us an ad and pointed out how there was a suggestive picture in the liquid being poured out of a bottle. I can still see the picture in my mind from all those years ago. God, is there a way to erase all this? How do we kick these unwanted images out of our minds?

Then the other night, God blessed me with an answer. He designed the most amazing, beautiful sunset I have ever seen! Taking a photo of it would not have done it any justice. I can't even describe it; it was just so miraculous. Now I have a wonderful memory that I can imagine in my head at any time. It was that powerful! And now I can use it as a weapon against any negative images that may try to come my way. Like Philippians 4:8 says:

Fix your thoughts on what is true and honorable and right, and pure and lovely and admirable. Think about things that are excellent and worthy of praise. (NLT)

Pornography distorts God's intended design of intimacy between a husband and a wife. Its heightening, numbing, and drugging effect on our senses is what people refer to as being "turned on." It's strong, but God is stronger. He has taught me, in James 4:7, how I should "submit to God, resist the devil and he will flee from me." In fact, I'm feeling some resistance as I write this. The devil does not want me sharing this with you, but here's what I say to him:

In the Name of Jesus, you must go and not be part of me again. I have no desire to go down your road ever again. I am going to stay on the road that is lit and straight. I am not going to hide the fact that you tried to get ahold of me before. I am being open and honest so that I may help others. Jesus has freed me from this, and He can free anyone else as well.

What Goes Around, Comes Around…

There are consequences to sin, and sometimes they are very serious. Pornography ruined our relationship as a couple. One day I finally drew the line and put an end to it, because I knew it was wrong. I felt so dirty, manipulated, and used. I was his wife and I wanted to please him, so I went along with all of it. But that is still no excuse. I needed to take responsibility for my part.

I should have stood my ground sooner. These memories have brought me back to high school when I didn't stand up to my boyfriend and lost my virginity. He said that if I loved him, I would have sex with him. So I did, and I didn't like it at all. It didn't feel very loving. When it ended, I immediately felt deep sorrow, and like I had done something very wrong. It wasn't this crazy, wonderful experience like it's always portrayed in the movies. I knew in my core that I shouldn't have done it. I should have said to him, "If *you* love *me*, then you will *wait* for me. I am not ready to do this now." Not speaking

28

up then, cost me dearly. And not speaking up sooner to my ex all these years later, cost me even more. Not only did it contribute to our separation, but it also caused me to suffer with terrible nightmares.

I only had those horrific dreams when I slept in that bed. Anytime I stayed at a friend's house I was blessed with wonderful restful sleep – no nightmares. But at home, I had terrible visions of being hooked up to machines, like when you're in the hospital. I would partially come out of the dreams, but I had to force myself to wake up and get out of the bed to prove that I could. Even when I did, the dreams were so real it felt like all the wires were still attached until I could get far enough away from the bed.

I think maybe because my ex-husband was an electrician, all those wires in my nightmares felt like he was hooking me up to them, trying to make me into a robot that would do whatever he programmed me to do. Thankfully, I was able to get up and escape the madness and get away from that bed… permanently.

God, thank You so much for Your Word, and for sharing Your great wisdom with us:

"People who conceal their sins will not prosper, but if they confess and turn from them, they will receive mercy." ~ Proverbs 28:13 (NLT)

Revealing this sin was the last thing I wanted to do. But it was the best thing for me. I don't have to carry along that tremendous amount of heavy weight anymore.

I'm so glad you did. You know I don't like to see you suffer. That is why I explain these things to you in My Word. I give you warnings about this type of sin:

"Don't you realize that those who do wrong will not inherit the Kingdom of God? Don't fool yourselves. Those who indulge in sexual sin, or who worship idols, or commit adultery, or are male prostitutes, or practice homosexuality, or are thieves, or greedy people, or drunkards, or are abusive, or cheat people — none of these will inherit the Kingdom of God. Some of you were once like that. But you were cleansed; you were

made holy; you were made right with God by calling on the name of the Lord Jesus Christ and by the Spirit of your God … Run from sexual sin! No other sin so clearly affects the body as this one does. For sexual immorality is a sin against your own body." ~ 1 Corinthians 6:9-11,18 (NLT)

Father, please forgive me for not only hurting myself, but I also tainted my relationship with You. I ask You to please cleanse me of this sin with my ex-husband, spiritually, physically, and emotionally. And while we're at it, Lord, all the other encounters I had while looking for love in all the wrong places, I bring those to you now.

Lord, I am so sorry! I must have really hurt You by my behavior. I want to be washed clean and free from all those secret sins. I want to warn others about all the hurts and heartaches that come from dabbling in sex, especially outside of marriage. We are taught about *birth* control protection, but nobody warns us that there is *no* protection available for our soul. I lost a little piece of mine each time I was with a man without being married to them. I regretted every one of them. I felt so dirty. Yet, I would find myself repeating the vicious cycle over and over again, hoping that there would be a different outcome — that I would have a man who would finally love me.

Oh, Lord, I thank You for sparing me from the consequence of an unplanned pregnancy, and then beyond that, from the consequences some girls suffer when they choose to get an abortion. They are fed lies about what exactly an abortion is doing, and they're not being told the truth that it is a baby that You have created inside of them. I know my heart goes out to all those women. I don't judge them in any way. They were lied to by the abortionists. I pray that they are given the opportunity to recover from it. Please show me if there are ways that I can help someone in their healing process.

Thank You for sparing me from that pain. Please forgive me, Father. I put men before You. You were the One who loved me all along, yet I crowded You out of my life and acted like I was no longer in a relationship with You. I let men be my "god" and would do anything they liked.

I forgive you, My Daughter. I just wish you never had gone through all that hurt and heartache. My ways are meant to keep you from these dangers and the pain they cause. It's because I love you, that I have given you all of the commandments in My Word — to protect you.

I designed marriage to be between a wife and husband who had not been intimate with anyone else, before each other. I understand how much hurt and pain are caused when two people who have joined themselves together as one, separate. There is a painful pulling apart. It is not a nice clean cut. It's a tearing of the souls. *That* is why I hate divorce, even if there is a very good reason for it, like abuse or unfaithfulness. Despite the fact that it may be a relief to end the relationship, the pain can still be felt in the soul.

Jesus, You know I struggled for years before ending my marriages, all those lists I made of reasons to stay versus reasons to go. It wasn't something that I decided overnight. Divorce was the last thing I wanted, but I found it was necessary and I know that You agreed with me, because You and I were in very close contact during those dark, confusing times. You gave me confirmation after confirmation. Thank You for rescuing me, Lord. And now thank You for cleansing me from all unrighteousness.

"But if we confess our sins to him, he is faithful and just to forgive us and to cleanse us from every wrong." ~ 1 John 1:9 (NLT)

"…throw off your old evil nature and your former way of life, which is rotten through and through, full of lust and deception. Instead, there must be a spiritual renewal of your thoughts and attitudes. You must display a new nature because you are a new person, created in God's likeness – righteous, holy, and true."

~ Eph. 4:22-24 (LRB)

"Because we have these promises, dear friends, let us cleanse ourselves from everything that can defile our body or spirit. And let us work toward complete holiness because we fear God."

~ 2 Corinthians 7:1 (LRB)

Tug of War...

It was very painful to go through the separation and eventual divorce of my marriage. It really felt like a constant tug of war. But it was far from being a game. This was a battle filled with arrows of lies, false guilt, accusations, and grief. Jesus teaches us in Matthew 19:5 that *the two shall become one flesh*. We had "tied the knot" and it would not untie very easily. It was more like ripping apart our flesh.

Part of my struggle was wondering if abuse and pornography were valid reasons to divorce. My abuser saw no reason, because he saw no problem with the pornography. In his mind, adultery or infidelity were the only true grounds for divorce, and he felt he wasn't guilty of either.

I looked up the word infidelity and it is defined as "a breach of trust" — not only the act of having an affair. A breach of trust can also occur when someone dishonors you repeatedly by abusing you emotionally. As difficult as it would be to experience the tearing apart, I knew that only then could the real healing begin.

Infidelity

Memories inside my head, they do not go
away. The sights, the sounds, impending
dread. Will they always stay?

Each day I wonder is this *really* how it
should be? I thought that Jesus came,
so we could live abundantly.

Abused and confused, is this all in my head?
Am I of the living, or of the living-dead?

I'm all torn up inside, please say this isn't so.
Is it true? Does God really want me to go?

Feeling like a child, who can't seem to get
it right. When I don't please the abuser,
then they begin to fight.

I live in fear if I don't do exactly as they say.
Putting my trust in the Creator as I move
ahead and pray.

Is it always with a fist that they use
as they attack? No, it's something that is gray.
It's not white and it's not black.

How do I explain what my life is like each day?
If I don't do as they please, then in some
way I will pay.

They give me no assurance — no respect,
as I deserve. As a follower of Christ,
it's *me* that they should serve.

Infidelity is defined as
"a breach of someone's trust."
Jesus says I should depart from there
and shake off all the dust.

Time is of the essence, it's time to live my life.
Even if that means, I'm no longer
someone's wife.

*"But in that coming day no weapon turned against
you will succeed. You will silence every voice raised
up to accuse you. These benefits are enjoyed by the*

servants of the LORD, their vindication will come from me. I, the LORD have spoken."
~ *Isaiah 54:17 (NLT)*

Then as God spoke these words of reassurance to me, He revealed that He, the *LORD*, is a
Lover **O**f **R**espect and **D**ignity:

My Daughter,

When there is continual abuse involved in any relationship, it is better for that relationship to end. That is not the way I want my children to be treated. And in some cases, it can be a matter of life or death. As you know, by My Word, you are meant to be loved and treated as I love and treat My church — with honor, grace, and respect — never by someone thoughtlessly exhibiting the desire to control another person, especially with threats.

I am a jealous God, which means that I despise seeing anyone being abused and mistreated; especially when the abuser tries to twist and turn the way that I think

of *you* into something negative. I want you to experience the unending, pure love I have for you.

Up until then, I was constantly second guessing myself and feeling that if I just prayed a little harder, things would get better. And if I were a better wife, then things would change. But it is impossible to please someone who continually changes the rules. Others have gone through the same madness and wondered how they could please an abuser, and then like me, discovered the truth – you can't.

From: Black & Blue
To: You

Did you ever get a slap in the face, bruised up and beaten, but no one touched you?

I have.

Did you ever feel like you were being hunted down like an innocent animal?

I have.

Did you ever feel like you were "drowning,"
in the many tears you were shedding?

I have.

Did you ever get judged, but not by what was
in your heart?

I have.

Did you ever get put down so often you began
to hang your head and feel worthless?

I have.

Have you ever "come above the water,"
that was caused by your own tears?

I have – you can too.

Have you ever let the Lord use those tears
to "water you" in order to grow?

I have – you can too.

Have you ever stopped blaming yourself
for how you were mistreated?

I have – you can too.

Have you ever depended upon Jesus and allowed *Him* to say who you really are?

I have – you can too.

Have you ever felt the peace and the presence of the Holy Spirit?

I have – you can too.

"He has made all things beautiful in its time…"
~ Ecclesiastes 3:11

Jesus, I firmly believe what the enemy wants to use against me, You can turn for good.[6] If I hadn't gone through those storms, even my stormy marriages, I wouldn't be able to lift other people up like I was lifted up.

You're right, and now you know what your 8:28 is from those marriages. I can use it to help others, like you wanted to do years ago. But it wasn't the right time. That has all changed now.

---

[6] Genesis 50:20

Now is when I will lift you up, so you can lift others up. You are ready. Look how far you have come. You have a heart to see not only victims of abuse helped, you're healed enough to want to help the abusers as well. I want that too. They are redeemable — both the men and the women who abuse others. If they truly come to repentance asking Me to forgive and cleanse them, I will rehabilitate them. They can become brand new people, too. I can make *all* things new, for nothing is impossible for Me!

"Let the redeemed of the Lord say so,
whom He has redeemed from the hand of the
enemy... with God all things are possible."

~ Psalm 107:2 & Matthew 19:26c

READY? HERE WE GO!

CHAPTER 3:

Hold on Tight

I'd like to take this page and maybe the next, to address something that I think we all deal with at one time or another, but for those who have been often told that "everything is their fault," it can happen more often than not.

I was scheduled to go on a mission's trip with a friend. Just prior to the trip, I ended up in the hospital with a bizarre injury and was unable to go. I was so disappointed. *Why did it have to happen? Is God punishing me? Did I do something wrong? Maybe I'm just not good enough to go.* Yet what happened next, made all my questions fade away.

My friend ended up taking her oldest son on the trip in my place. As sad as I felt, I got some incredible news from her that turned it all around for me. God did an 8:28. While they were there, her son decided to ask Jesus to be His Savior and committed his life to following God's lead! Not only that, but him being there saved his mother's life too: As she was crossing the street, he was able to pull her back out of the way of an oncoming truck heading straight for her.

Would those events have happened if he had stayed home during that time? I doubt it. I think he needed to be right where he was at exactly that time, and under those unique circumstances. And it made all my pain and disappointment melt away to know that my temporary "trial" was a part of someone else's eternal, miraculous event.

Did God cause my injury? I don't believe so. It was an unexplainable one, so I know it wasn't natural. The loving God I serve is a Healer, and Jesus already took all my punishment for sin on the Cross. So it wasn't punishment. God is a good, good Father and He would never inflict injury or sickness on any of His kids.

But in this world, we have trials. And we learn and grow stronger through them. We learn from natural consequences (i.e. stoves are hot, ice is slippery) and those lessons can be hard. Sometimes our bad choices cause us suffering or they affect someone else. We all experience having to live with the consequences of other people's sin. That's where forgiveness comes in, and the healing power of Jesus' Blood. But this injury that kept me home was obviously none of those. God showed me that He can redeem and heal anything the enemy throws at us.

With all that said, I mentioned earlier that I had such a hard time trying to put my finger on the abuse because the emotional part of abuse *isn't black or white, it's so... gray.* For those in a similar situation, I trust they will understand what I mean by that. But when you add God to the equation, "gray" can take on a whole new meaning:

GRAY = God **R**edeems **A**ll **Y**esterdays.

I hope that these verses I'm about to share will bring some relief. I find comfort and healing in God's Word and I enjoy doing what I call "Bible Digging." I begin by looking up a verse. Then, as I am searching for it, I find other verses highlighted on other pages and they, too, usually speak to my situation and I can't get enough of His Word, I keep digging for more and more. These following Scripture verses were discovered during one of my many "excavations."

I started with **Psalm 34:15, 17-18** (LRB):

> *"The eyes of the LORD watch over those who do right; His ears are open to their cries for help ... The LORD hears His people when they call to Him for help. He rescues them from all their troubles. The LORD is close to the broken-hearted, He rescues those who are crushed in spirit."*

Which led me to **Psalm 37** (LRB):

> *"Trust in the LORD and do good, then you will*

live safely in the land and prosper. Take delight in the LORD, and He will give you your heart's desires. Commit everything you do to the LORD, trust Him, and He will help you. He will make your innocence as clear as the dawn, and the justice of your cause will shine like the noonday sun." **(Verses 3-6)**

"It is better to be godly and have little, than to be evil and possess much. For the strength of the wicked will be shattered, but the LORD takes care of the godly. Day by day the LORD takes care of the innocent, and they will receive a reward that lasts forever. They will survive through hard times, even in famine they will have more than enough." **(Verses 16-19)**

"The steps of the godly are directed by the LORD. He delights in every detail of their lives. Though they stumble, they will not fall, for the LORD holds them by the hand." **(Verses 23-24)**

Don't be impatient for the LORD to act! Travel steadily along His path, He will honor you, giving you the land. You will see the wicked destroyed." **(Verse 34)**

Then on to **Psalm 55:16-23** (LRB):

"…I will call on God, and the LORD will rescue me. Morning, noon, and night I plead aloud in my distress, and the LORD hears my voice. He rescues me and keeps me safe from the battle waged against me, even though many still oppose me. God who is king forever, will hear me and will humble them. For my enemies refuse to change their ways; they do not fear God. As for this friend of mine, he betrayed me; he broke his promises. His words are as smooth as cream, but in his heart is war. His words are as soothing as lotion, but underneath are daggers! Give your burdens to the LORD, and He will take care of you. He will not permit the godly to slip and fall …I am trusting You to save me."

These verses inspired me to write the following acronym because I was dealing with fear in moving forward:

FEAR = **F**orget **E**very **&** **A**ll **R**ejections.

Father, with Your help, I am going to try to live that out. Lord, You know it is my prayer that

50

by exposing the lies and madness I went through, I want to reach any person in a similar situation, and help them to know that they are not the one who is crazy.

God provided me with the support group, Celebrate Recovery. As I met with a small, intimate group of women, we were each able to share our deep, dark secrets and were not met with any judgment — only support. Having an understanding counselor was also very helpful. Getting someone else's point of view of the situation helped me to conclude that I wasn't responsible for the abuser's actions, and I was not making all of it up. It was my reality that I was discovering. And now was the time to move forward.

Moving Forward

In the past, when I'd been gone from him,
bad times would start to fade. I'd start to
question my move, and if I should have stayed.
I feel bad for him, because now he's all alone —
No one there to greet him, at night
when he comes home.

I know I should forgive the man
who's caused me so much strife.
It's the only way I can move on —
to get on with my life.

It's okay to be away from him;
I did not need to stay.
God's helped me to move forward now;
He's shown me there's a way.

When that man speaks down to me,
next time I will not cower. It's the Lord
who will sustain me — the One
who'll give me power.

There's a time for every season —
a time I should move on.
Christ's given me permission to.
This time I will be strong.

*"God is our refuge and strength, a very present
help in trouble. Therefore, we will not fear...
The Lord of hosts is with us. The God of Jacob
is our refuge." ~ Psalm 46:1-2,7*

I am going to go forward by stepping out in

FAITH = Forge **A**head **I**n **T**rust **&** **H**ope.

I'm reminded of the story of Joshua and the Israelites when they finally were crossing the Jordan river into their Promised land. Those leaders had to step by faith into the river and actually get their feet wet in order for the waters to divide and allow the people to move forward, (unlike in Exodus when God parted the Red Sea *before* they stepped in).

The time has come for us, like Joshua, and we need to be brave enough to get our feet wet. Trusting in our God means we don't need to see how everything is going to work out; we just need to faithfully keep moving forward one step at a time, knowing that He is there guiding us all the way.

I made a vow to God. I told Him I would do whatever He wanted me to do with my life. I made a commitment to Him. Two weeks later, I had the courage to leave my unhealthy marriage. And boy, was God with me as I went through the process of getting a divorce! I have absolutely no doubt that I did the right thing. I had struggled with that decision for years and it was a relief to finally have it resolved. I was at peace again, no longer having nightmares.

Wide Awake

Here I am now, wide awake. Had been
abused, for goodness' sake. Because You
were there, You helped me get through.
Helping others is what I will do.

It's true, You can make good,
come out of the bad. You heal us, Oh Lord —
I am no longer sad. Sometimes the bad,
can become something new. Sorrow to joy,
is something You do.

Understanding the pain, we'll help out
the others, letting them know they're Your
sons and Your daughters.

I've forgiven him Lord, but I don't want to
forget, so I can help out the others, who've
been caught in that net.

I know he hurts too, from all his dysfunction.
Ignoring the pain — just so he can function.
Loud and overbearing, he thinks
he's real tough. But You'll let him know
when You've had enough.

Low self-esteem with a serious face.
He needs You, dear Lord, to show him
Your grace. Even to You, he still may say "no."
I give him to You God; it's time I let go.

Sometimes we eat to deal with the pain.
Sometimes we drink, it's all just the same.
Gently and lovingly, You can bring
them all back; helping them learn,
from all their attacks.

My dream, dear Lord, is to be used by You.
I only need You, for this dream to come true.
Lord, we're ready now. Today is the day.
We want to move on — to make a new way.

We'll hear Jesus calling, and we'll be heard too.
Free from abuse, we'll all be brand new.

*"The LORD will fight for you, and you shall
hold your peace." ~ Exodus 14:14*

To the one who has been abused: You'll get to the point when "who you are" has disappeared and died. But Jesus offers the hope that you *can* and *will* live in peace again. It can even begin right here, right now:

"I am the resurrection and the life. He who believes in Me, though he may die, he shall live ... This is the message from the One who is holy and true. He is the One who has the key of David. He opens doors, and no one can shut them; He shuts doors, and no one can open them. I know all the things you do, and I have opened a door for you that no one can shut. You have little strength, yet you obeyed My word and did not deny Me. Look! I will force those who belong to Satan ... to come and bow down at your feet. They will acknowledge that you are the ones I love...

Because you have kept My command to persevere, I also will keep you from the hour of trial which shall come upon the whole world, to test those who dwell on the earth. Behold, I am coming quickly! Hold fast what you have, that no one may take your crown. He who overcomes, I will make him a pillar in the temple of My God, and he shall go out no more. I will write on him the name of My God and the name of the city of My God, the New Jerusalem, which comes down out of heaven from My God. And I will write on him My new name. He who has an ear, let him hear what the Spirit says to the churches." [7]

Remember this:
I know your heart and I love you!

"It is better to be godly and have little, than to be evil and possess much. For the strength of the wicked will be shattered, but the LORD takes care of the godly. Day by day the LORD takes care of the innocent, and they will receive a reward that lasts forever. They will survive through hard times, even in famine they will have more than enough." [8]

Oh, Lord, my God, and my Father, I could quote from Your Word all day long. I thirst for it and

---

[7] John 11:25, Revelation 3:7-8 (LRB), Revelation 3:10-13

[8] Psalm 37:16-18 (LRB)

can't get enough. It pleases me so much! It makes me feel closer to You the more I read it. I fully believe that You will give me a new chance at living in victory. I truly believe that Christ has a new name, and a new identity for me. You've made it possible for me to go from being "Sorry" to being "Significant." It might take a while to fully grasp that truth, but I believe I am significant in Your eyes.

Significant

This is not what I intended when I said to him,
"I do." But now that it's over, it's God
who'll see me through.

My head had been spinning, trying to please
that man each day. It's Jesus who told me:

**"Honey, there's just not a way.
Let Me be your Teacher. Let Me be
your Guide. Together we will do this;
you no longer need to hide."**

But in church they keep saying
divorce isn't the way.

58

**"Let them walk in your shoes...
for just one day."**

A "basket case" I had been called
by my spouse. I'll never go back —
not go to that house.

**"My daughter, it's true —
you're significant in My eyes.
You can move on now, it's time;
get away from the lies.**

**I have greater plans for you,
don't doubt it one minute.
From your trials will come joy
if you just keep Me in it."**

*"...when He, the Spirit of truth, has come,
He will guide you into all truth; For He
will not speak on His own authority,
but whatever He hears He will speak;
And He will tell you things to come."*

~ John 16:13

We needn't go far to discover there are others
suffering right alongside us. We'll realize that

we are more alike than we can imagine. Many of us have been cheated and hurt and lied to for so long, it has made trusting anyone so very hard to do. We have been made to believe that we are crazy and don't know anything. Hope of us escaping our situation seems slim. I am here to tell you: I found there is a way.

I know full well what it's like to feel numb. I was downcast physically as well as emotionally. It was all encompassing and affected me in so many ways. I found it difficult to be in social situations. I was always trying to blend into the background, so I wouldn't have to talk to anyone. I feared that they might find out who I really was. Scared and unsure of myself, I even made-up excuses to protect the abuser.

Even in a safe environment with a counselor I trusted, mustering up the strength to talk and share was still difficult. I went through an experience of not being able to breathe. It felt as if all my air was caught in my chest, and I couldn't find my voice because I had not been allowed to speak. I had been silent for way too long.

Then one day it all changed. I found the other people who were in the trenches with me. There were times that even in that safe support group it was hard to get the words out. It was difficult, at first, yet as I heard the others tell their stories and realized I was not alone, the words began to rise… but got stuck. The pressure built, and so did my determination to find my voice to let it out. I took a deep breath, and out the words poured. And even though I was embarrassed, I could breathe again, and I felt somewhat lifted.

I am here to tell you that there is hope. I discovered that Jesus has been right there in the bunker with us all along. He is the One who gives us the strength and the will to keep getting up in order to survive. We are mighty warriors in this battle – and **we will *not* be overcome.**

When we hear in the book of Matthew that the meek will inherit the earth, we can't understand how that could be. Being meek gives us the notion that we are weak. That is far from the truth. The definition of meek is: *great strength* under control. The Bible is full of heroes who were characterized as meek: Abraham, Moses,

David, and even Jesus.

We are told to submit our lives to the will of God. Now, that may sound scary after what we have been through, but when we do let go and trust our Heavenly Father, we learn that it is for our own benefit. When we "let go" we think we have to blindly fall *backwards*, nervously hoping Jesus will catch us. Not so. We are able to fall *forward* into His loving arms and be held and loved by Him.

In the book of Zephaniah, we can find much hope and encouragement:

> *"Sing, O daughter of Zion … Be glad and rejoice with all your heart, O daughter of Jerusalem! … At last, your troubles will be over, and you will never again fear disaster. On that day the announcement to Jerusalem will be, "Cheer up, Zion! Don't be afraid For the LORD your God is living among you. He is a mighty savior.*
>
> *He will take delight in you with gladness. With His love, He will calm all your fears. He will rejoice over you with joyful songs … you will be disgraced no more.*

And I will deal severely with all who have oppressed you. I will save the weak and helpless ones; I will bring together those who were chased away. I will give glory and fame to my former exiles, wherever they have been mocked and shamed. On that day, I will gather you together and bring you home again. I will give you a good name, a name of distinction among all the nations of the earth as I restore your fortunes before their very eyes. I, the LORD have spoken!"

~ Zephaniah 3:14-20 (NLT)

I speak from my own experience that it has lessened my pain by journaling and seeing my counselor. The more I write and go over what the Holy Spirit has led me to, the more freedom I gain. I will remember, Christ is my Healer, and He **will restore me!!!** Recovering from my pain is possible:

"Therefore, behold, I will allure her, will bring her into the wilderness, and speak comfort to her. I will give her vineyards from there, and

the Valley of Achor[9] as a door of hope; she shall
sing there, as in the days of her youth, as in the
day when she came up from the land of Egypt.
"And it shall be, in that day," says the LORD,
"That you will call Me 'My Husband,' and no
longer call Me 'My Master.' ~ Hosea 2:14-16

Father, I remember when You spoke to me
through that dream: *I was standing on the lip of*
a huge chalkboard, walking across from the left to
the right, holding onto the wall for dear life. As I did,
there were words of discouragement all over it,
words like: loser, you're ugly, you're no good. Once
I got to the end of the board, I began to walk from
the right back to the left. This time was different
though. There were words again, but they had
changed to positive and encouraging words like:
you're beautiful, you are kind, you are worthy.

It was around 2:00 AM when I awoke, and I
felt such peace. I also felt empowered to move
away from the marriage to my first husband.

---

[9] "Achor" in Hebrew can mean: trouble, gloomy,
dejected or affliction

Unlike the negative words I was used to hearing from him, I felt like You were telling me through this dream who I really was in Your sight, and that You love me just as I am. The peace you sent to me gave me the strength I needed to face what was really happening in my failing marriage. Knowing how much You love me, helped me let go of the past.

There is hope for restoration for all of us — as though we had never been tarnished. Our joy will be all-encompassing:

"So, I will restore to you the years that the swarming locusts have eaten …

You shall eat in plenty and be satisfied, and praise the name of the Lord your God, who has dealt wondrously with you; and My people shall never be put to shame.

Then you shall know that I am in the midst of Israel; I am the Lord your God and there is no other. My people shall never be put to shame."

~ Joel 2:25-27

Restore

Before I left, I was depressed as could be.
I was dreaming those dreams,
like nightmares to me.

Oppression was something I felt
right to the core. "That's it!" I said,
"I can't take anymore."

With my stomach in knots, I even forgot
how to breathe. I packed up my things;
it was the last time I'd leave.

Four times I'd left — seemed like
once every season. Something told me:
there must be a reason.

Now that I'm gone, I can sleep
well again. No tossing & turning,
it's come to an end.

Survive on my own is something
I'll do. Jesus reminds me,
"I'm always with you."

Now is the time that I move on from here.
I am learning full well I have nothing to fear.

Being faithful to Christ is what
I strive for. No more crying & weeping,
life holds so much more.

I'm able to say now that He is my Savior.
There's so much in life I'd now like to savor.

*"Restore to me the joy of Your salvation, and
uphold me by Your generous Spirit."*

~ Psalm 51:12

3: Hold on Tight

CHAPTER 4:
Following the Leader

Moving ahead through those dark valleys and hard rocky places would have been impossible without the Good Shepherd leading (and on some days carrying) me. But with God on my SeeSaw, what I've noticed as I read through my journals is that for every "down" I endure, He blesses me two or three times over to lift my spirits back up again:

> I asked the man next door if he would be willing to help me load my furniture onto the moving truck I would be driving. Then, I asked my friend whose basement I'm using to store most of my things, if she knew of

a neighbor on her end who could help.
Praise God! The answer was yes on both ends.
I then called U-Haul and booked the truck.
I'll be moving out in two days (the last day
before he will be changing the locks).

Oh Lord, "I waited patiently for You
and You inclined Your ear toward me." [10]
If I may be so bold, can You hold off the
rain while we are moving? Thanks!

After booking the U-Haul, they told me
they require a $150 deposit (cash) at the
time of pick-up. I don't have enough in my
account. I put my trust in God; everything
will work out — it always does. I need to just
trust and obey. Later, I called Mom to see
if she could check the mail. She told me that
I received a check for $295. It was money
that I was owed that I had forgotten about
— not only did I get what I needed for the
deposit, God gifted me with an abundance
of help! The Lord's timing is so perfect!

~~~

---

[10] Psalm 40:1

I went to the house and took apart my daybed ALL BY MYSELF, which was a big accomplishment for me. I was ready to move on (in more ways than one). I felt my SeeSaw rising up from the ground to a more balanced place.

~~~

MOVING DAY!
Picked up the U-Haul and met my neighbor at the house. It took us 1½ hours to load up the truck. It was packed so tightly that I had to leave my sewing machine and my "hopeless" chest behind; they just wouldn't fit. Then I went to my friend's house. She had lunch ready for us. We hung around until the neighbor arrived at 3:00 PM. We loaded the cellar and finished at 4:00 PM.

Thank You, Jesus, for holding off the rain today as we moved. I was so happy that it was only snowing lightly with no accumulation.

I told my support group that I was getting a divorce and they confirmed that my decision was justified, which brought me

71

great relief. They were truly supportive,
unlike others who met me with judgmental
condemnation, even saying that I was out
of God's will and quoting scriptures to me.

Disillusioned

My friends, I thought, would always stay.
As I divorce, they start to stray.
Forgive them, Lord, they just don't know,
That as they leave, they hurt me so.

Disillusioned — in so much pain —
yet through it all, I find You reign.

Don't you think that I have tried?
I've been abused, torn up inside.
He goes to church, tells them all those lies.
He conned them all; and so was I.

Disillusioned — in so much pain —
yet through it all, I find You reign.

Now God's released me from all those snares,
I'm moving forward with no more cares.
Much less money, I now possess.
It's worth it all — I now can rest.

"He heals the brokenhearted and binds up their wounds. He counts the number of the stars; He calls them all by name. Great is our LORD, and mighty in power; His understanding is infinite. The LORD lifts up the humble; He casts the wicked down to the ground." ~ Psalm 147:3-6

~~~

Today when I went to Celebrate Recovery, it was very productive and joyful, and God really was present! Once I was home, I rearranged my bedroom so I could put my computer in there. I hooked all the wires up myself — and it worked! Another victory!

~~~

I was in a gift shop that was having a big sale. They put a large sign out on the sidewalk stating that. I came across a beautiful ring, with a light green stone and "diamonds" around it. I really liked it, and it fit great, so I bought it. It wasn't until later, that I realized it was my birthstone. I got it for myself to wear on my wedding band finger to represent my new life.

I spoke to my friend who is also going

through a divorce from an abusive husband.
I truly believe that God has put us together
to get us through this time, with support
from each other. We have shared Scripture
verses and also our experiences. She said
she's had a couple of good days; they have
been filled with joy. I know what she means;
that is how I have been feeling.

He called yesterday and today. I didn't
take his calls or return them. I have moved
everything out and there is no reason for me
to have to communicate with him. As far as
I'm concerned, we are ALREADY divorced.

~~~

Lord, God, if You want this pain to be used
to help others, please send me where You
desire.

~~~

Sold my wedding rings today.

~~~

Filed divorce papers with the superior court.
The substantial fees which I couldn't afford
were waived! Thank You, God!

~~~

I discovered that I only had $5.00 left to my name; I sat down and cried, trying to figure out what I was going to do. I couldn't ask my family for anything because they have already been providing me with housing and food, so I ended up calling the church and explained my situation. They said they would contact the Deacons, and someone would get back to me. After explaining my situation to him, he said that I could meet someone at the church tomorrow at noon. They would give me some food vouchers. Oh, Lord God, I'll say it again: You are my awesome Provider! Now I'm trusting You about my prescription.

Then He reminded me that I had a can with change in it. I was able to get $20 out of it — enough to put toward my prescription. Thank You, Jesus, for helping me.

~~~

After I got back in the car from paying for my prescription with so many dimes and

quarters, the tears started back up.
I composed myself because I was going
to go to the grocery store with the vouchers
from the church, but I just couldn't; I started
to cry all over again, because of the reality
that I had to ask for this help.

~~~

I was still having a difficult time and was
not able to relax. A friend suggested that
I put on a Christian radio station, as I slept.
Then when I woke up during the night,
I was blessed by hearing the lyrics to a song,
which said:
    "God will take care of you... through
  everyday... o'er all the way. He will care for
     you... God will take care of you."
I peacefully went back to sleep.
Coincidence? No... it's a God-incidence!

~~~

I went to my appointment with my
counselor. She said I could pay the co-pay
next month. And my psychiatrist said not to
cancel appointments with him because of not

76

being able to pay the co-pay, that something could be worked out. More blessings from You, Lord. You are my awesome Provider, Teacher, and Friend!

~~~

Went to Sunday Service and the pastor was talking about how difficult the holidays are for some people. I couldn't hold the tears back. I feel so bad that he is all alone right now, and probably will be for Christmas. I still want nothing to do with him, but it hurts me to see someone lonely — that is one of the saddest things.

~~~

He received the divorce papers and texted me. I didn't respond. I found my voice by not using it!

~~~

Lord, I know that Your Word says to rest in You and wait patiently, but sometimes it is so difficult. I pray for your perseverance and grace. Thank You, Lord.

~~~

Tonight, he texted me, saying that he and
the cats missed me. I have not responded
to any of his texts or calls over the last few
weeks. But tonight, I found it necessary to
respond by simply texting back STOP!
I did not hear from him after that.

~~~

I was going to drop off a Thank You note
to the man who helped me move, and also
to see if I could get in the house to get my
sewing machine. But as I was approaching
the road that the house was on, my stomach
started tying like knots again. I just couldn't
do it. I don't ever want to go there again.
I'll gladly leave the pieces of furniture behind
— as long as I can move forward.

~~~

I had a party to thank family for helping
me to move, and also for their listening ears
concerning my marital problems over the
years. We celebrated me moving on with
the divorce. After everyone left tonight there
was a song on the radio which said:

"We are beautiful, no matter what they say...
Words won't bring us down ... so don't you
bring me down today." [11]

Lord, I am so thankful for Your presence in
my life. It is so wonderful to be excited about
life again. Praise be to our Lord God
Almighty, to Jesus, and His Holy Spirit!

God showed Himself to me in many mighty ways as I went through two court cases, in two different courthouses, at the same time. I was in the process of getting the divorce from my abusive marriage at one, while I was needing to file a modification against my first husband (regarding custody) at another. The Lord was walking me step-by-step through both of them with His endless supply of wisdom. He guided me in asking the right questions. And if I didn't get a satisfactory answer, He moved me in another direction until I was satisfied.

Even so, I was doubting myself the day I went

---

[11] *Beautiful* written by Linda Perry, performed by
Christina Aguilera 2002

into the courthouse to pursue the modification. But God had not left my side. When I went downstairs to get change for the copy machine, Jesus was there waiting to give me a surprise gift: the people running the café told me that they were born-again Christians. We hugged and we were instantly bonded. They also had Christian music piped through their sound system. I stayed and relaxed in the presence of God's grace and mercy and the soothing music. When I rose to leave, they asked if we could pray first. Of course, I said yes!

The next time I was there, as I prepared my modification papers, a woman leaned over and said, "If you need any help, let me know — I'm *bored*! I'm just waiting for them to find my paperwork." Come to find out, she was an attorney. After she looked over my paperwork, she gave me her card and said, "But you don't need a lawyer; you're doing just fine!" *Was that a real person Lord or did you send me an angel?*

Then on another day, I went back to that same courthouse to check on things, and they gave me a form to fill out called "Request for Pre-

Trial Hearing." The clerk checked off the box: "earliest possible trial date" — without me even asking.

While I was there, I had the opportunity to go to the café again. The woman there who had prayed with me before, waited on me. I paid her for my Danish with coins and then asked how much the water cost. I pulled some change out of my pocket (about 38¢) and she said, "That's okay, that's enough." Two blessings in one day.

God Bless this Mess

In regards to my divorce case, when I went to the courthouse to file, they handed me a "Do-it-Yourself Divorce" packet. Overwhelming as it was, that is exactly what I did!

The night before I went to court regarding alimony, I had a dream:

Gramma and I were joking around, and I gave a smart-aleck answer to her question. She then laughed and reached out and pulled me close. As we embraced, my head buried in her big bosom,

I felt her telling me that it was okay to be "a little feisty" (something I needed to get permission to do, because both men would tell me I was mentally unstable anytime I challenged them and stood up for my rights). *Hugging her and not wanting to let go, I cried and said, "Gramma, I miss you so much!"* I find comfort knowing she is waiting for me in heaven.

When I awoke, I knew that everything was going to be okay. I went to the alimony hearing feeling "a little feisty." I had gotten to know the security marshals pretty well by then; they looked out for me, and they put me at ease when I arrived. Since my soon-to-be ex did not show up, I was awarded a substantial amount of money. I also was able to attach it to his wages. He was "not pleased" when he found out, and it led to an alimony *modification* hearing.

Little did I know when the hearing date arrived, that I was about to be blessed, yet again, on my trail of trials. As I sat in the one and only room of the courthouse that had chairs, eating my peanut butter and jelly sandwich, he and his attorney walked in and sat at a desk nearby.

He never saw me there. I guess the Lord gave me a front-row seat to hear them going over his case. I was able to hear 90% of what they were saying, including when the attorney said in a hopeless tone of voice, "Oh boy, she doesn't have any money!"

I actually heard him say to her that he didn't know why we were getting divorced. I guess he forgot that he took off his wedding ring one day, and also the fact that he stood up and walked out in the middle of our last marriage counseling session. Hearing all that confirmed for me, as trying as this trial was, God was *with* me and *for* me and would somehow work everything together for my good. Another 8:28 was in progress!

Little blessings and confirmations along the way mean so much as we add them up. Like when I went to the town hall to get a printout of what I requested. It was a dollar per page, so I owed them nine dollars. Turned out, it was exactly what I had left in my pocket! I know it seems like a small thing, but it was a reminder to me that God cares about every little detail.

All those "small" blessings gave me courage to face the bigger challenges, like what happened next.

It had been my plan to follow along with the "Do-it-Yourself Divorce," but things drastically changed when he hired an attorney. I was *very* uncomfortable about going to court against the two of them, so I began a search for a pro-bono attorney (I didn't have the money to hire anyone). For two days I was on the phone calling one attorney after another, telling my story, and asking for representation. Finally, I reached an attorney, who offered a free consultation. I set up an appointment for the next week. Success! God brought me the help I needed!

Thank You, Jesus! You're so good! Following Your lead always pays off. You have taught me to have patience, perseverance, and to *keep on knocking* on the doors and not accept "no" for an answer — to keep speaking up for my rights. I have finally found my voice! You are a mighty and awesome Savior, and I hope the world can see Your presence through me and these *trials* (literally - two court cases)!

God continued to bless me over and over along the trail with sweet surprises. One day, there were about 20 robins outside the kitchen window, on the ground and in the holly bush, and also in a little bare tree. It was amazing! It made me smile. Like the promise of spring, I took it as a little sign from God that I was in His will, going through both of those court cases. My family and a few of my truest friends were so supportive and encouraging! They had wanted me to leave him years ago.

Though their support made it bearable, the stress of it all affected my body and I needed to see a chiropractor. They sent me first to get x-rays done of my back at the hospital. On my way out, walking by the hospital gift shop, I saw their flowers for sale. Since it was Valentine's Day time, I bought myself an arrangement in a little mug. It had a pink rose, white daisies, and pink mini-carnations (in colors that I liked, not in the color *he* liked and always insisted on).

Later, I wrote in my journal:

> This has been the best Valentine's Day I have ever had!
>
> After church I went to a theater in the city on Main Street. It was an open reception for a very successful and sweet woman who was turning 80 years old. She is the woman who founded the homeless shelter where I had once stayed. [More about that later.] She is the sweetest woman, but she doesn't get pushed around. She stands up for what she believes in. She is someone I admire and would like to learn from.
>
> At the entrance they were collecting tickets for the show which would be following the reception. Seeing the tickets were $48 and out of my price range, I told them I was only going to the reception, and they let me in. I spoke with many people who I knew there. I was so glad to see an old friend, the director of the women's center that I used to go to. She asked me where I would be sitting, and I told her I wasn't going to the show. "Oh yes you are. I have an extra

ticket!" She handed it to me and said she would see me inside after the reception. Once inside, we were talking, and she asked me if I had any plans after the show. There would be one empty seat now at her dinner table because the guest whose ticket I was using was unable to attend, so would I like to come?

On the way to her house, I stopped at a flower stand. A dozen roses were $25 and the ½ dozen roses were $20. I went to my wallet and asked if I could have one rose for $5. She said, "I'll do even better than that — $5 for ½ dozen!" An offer I could not pass up! And I was able to pass the blessing along to my dinner-hostess friend.

God, I love all the ways you surprise me with so many unexpected gifts! If anyone were to ask me to be their Valentine, my response would be: "The only One I will be a Valentine to this year is God. He is all I need and want!" Thank you, Lord, for one of the best days of my life!

Here are a few last journal entries that were

written in the middle of it all when my SeeSaw was teeter-tottering full tilt. Looking back now I can see that all along the way, my God was with me, preparing me for my next assignment:

What a day Lord. I thank You for all of it — even the hurt. I pray that I am able to glorify Your Name through all of this pain and suffering.

~~~

Lord God, thank You for bringing people into my life who are positive. My divorcing friend came over and we not only made earrings together, but we shared a lot. We are both feeling called to speak in front of others (Celebrate Recovery, for example — but even beyond that). I really feel down deep in my soul, that the Lord would like me to minister to those who are in abusive relationships. And, furthermore, to educate pastors about abuse, and that there ARE times when someone should be allowed to leave even their Christian marriage.

~~~

The Lord woke me this morning by showing me that all my life experiences will be put together to do His work; that each piece is part of His grander scheme.

Lord, now I am trusting You completely. I have been trying to squelch the call You have on my life. I am now fully committed and ready to follow You on the path You have laid out for me. I surrender all, Jesus!

Standing by My Convictions

Stand by your convictions and leave
the rest to Me. Tell the truth in love,
so that all of them may see.

The world has gone crazy, it's all
upside down. With Me by your side,
we'll erase every frown.

I'm in control of this world, it's still
precious to Me. Give me your faith,
and soon you'll be free.

You can trust in My promise because
I am the King. Before you know it,
you'll find you can sing.

Following Me will bring joy
to your heart, and love will grow
and heal every part.

Let Me be your Hero, if you're
feeling lost. I'll help you find your voice,
when you're being crossed.

Others have hurt you, but with Me
there's no doubt; Honor and respect,
is what I'm all about.

I created you for more, when you
were just a seed. I've so much planned for you
and I'll give you all you need.

Trusting in Me is how I want you
to live. And soon you'll find out —
you have so much to give.

Your mission is to help those who have gone
through the same. Abused or unbalanced
can be healed by My Name.

So, take all the lessons I have been
teaching to you; Just stay with Me —
that's how you'll get through.

*The LORD replied, "I will personally
go with you..." ~ Exodus 33:14 (LRB)*

CHAPTER 5:
Tagged...
But Not Out

There are some things our body remembers how to do without us even thinking about it. It is called muscle memory. "It's like riding a bike." Yet there are things we would rather *not* remember, but our body just won't let us forget, like how it feels falling *off* the bike: hitting the ground hard, scraping our knees and elbows, and then having to clean them. Ouch!

If you have never ridden a bike, it's hard to relate, I know. What I'm about to share with you in this chapter, I'm only sharing to help you understand how it can feel to be labeled or tagged with a mental "illness" like bipolar disorder or catatonia. If someone you know and love is dealing with the extreme emotional ups and downs of depression, anxiety, sensory overload, hypersensitivity, or over-excitedness, I thought it might be helpful if I describe what I experienced from this side of things for so many years. Even if you have not been "diagnosed" you may be able to relate to the common feelings and responses we all have to some degree. It is just that in many cases, especially with post trauma, these feelings intensify and feel out of control.

After being made to believe by narcissistically abusive people that I was mentally unstable, I had lost my voice. It was hard to put into words what was happening in my head. But now I'm ready to. For anyone who has been on a SeeSaw like mine, you may find comfort seeing that it is not just you, you're not alone. I pray that the healing presence of our Shepherd who has walked me through, will be felt by you as you read this.

If you're sensitive to such things, you may choose to skip over this chapter altogether, and that's okay. I just feel compelled that someone, somewhere, will benefit from hearing this part of my story:

Amplified!

This is a story, strange, but true. We're
more than our label, we're kind of like you.
We're parents and daughters, and sons,
just the same. Yet, we struggle and feel
that we're going insane.

Sometimes we wonder is it us,
or the world? Because our mind keeps on
racing; it's caught in a twirl: Look at this!
Look at that! Buy now! — hurry, hurry!
How did we survive, before all of this flurry?

Things are amplified, much larger than life.
We can't help all these troubles, problems,
and strife. To you it's one thing, to us it's
another, 'cause to us it's ten times,
when to you it's no bother.

We want you to know that we feel lots of pain.
But for us, it's what's called
"cramps in the brain."

Keep in touch with the doctor — stay on meds,
just the same. That's what we do
to stay basically sane.

What can you do for people like us?
Be patient, be gentle, be prayerful and trust.

Bipolar makes life seem too dark
or too bright. With God's assistance,
He'll make things all right.

*"I will say of the LORD, He is my refuge and
fortress; my God, in Him I will trust."*
~ Psalm 91:2

Living with a diagnosis of bipolar, a chemical imbalance, chronic depression, schizophrenia, obsessive-compulsive disorder, or any other "serious" label, can leave us in a constant state of fear. We fear being misunderstood, locked up, sent away, or shamed. Place someone like that in an abusive marriage, and it's downright terrifying.

Why Can't I?

I have feelings of my own, I'm just like you,
Even if I have, a different point of view.
You raise your voice, tell me how I am bad.
Being treated that way, can make me real sad.

Don't say a word, stuff it deep down inside.
Keep your cool, don't divert, or it's an
ambulance ride. I want to be balanced
and stay healthy too. Why can't I think
something that's different from you?

I can't be perfect, and I can't always please.
Expressing my view, is tough with this disease.
If I get mad, even a little upset, don't send
me away; I'm not ready just yet.

My anger has truth, I must get it out.
If I keep it all in, at some point I'll shout!
I've been walking on eggshells, never
making a sound. My emotions aren't flat,
they go up, they go down.

Be patient with me; mistakes I will make,
Not one of us is perfect, for heaven's sake.

I'm trying to learn how to stay healthy
and sane. God's there in the sun,
and He's there in the rain.

Don't need your permission to have
something to say. I'm learning more skills,
as I go through each day. Gramma gave me
permission "to be feisty" — it's true.
I'm done pleasing people — only Jesus will do.

Christ got loud – even threw tables
on the floor. I'm not going to be quiet...
no longer. No more!

"For God has not given us a spirit of fear, but of
power and of love and of a sound mind."
~ 2 Timothy 1:7

Somebody
Turn
Off the
Power!

Note: The following was written in April of 2004. The intensity described has only increased since then. It greatly affects us all, but some people more so, than others.

Have you ever had way too much caffeine in your system? Your mind, and usually your voice too, are on super speed; you cannot stop talking, and you begin to climb the walls looking for a way to find something to do with the excessive energy racing around inside of you. That partly describes what mania can be like. It is frustrating when I'm not able to "shut off" my brain and I have so much energy that I'm climbing the walls.

The world we live in is always ON. Our power comes from the *outside,* instead of from *within.* Our heads are still spinning even when we do stop and turn OFF the noise. It may be even scary to have things quiet; it can sometimes actually "hurt" because the quiet can be so "loud." It doesn't make sense, but it's true. It's because of our minds trying to shut off.

The chaos of our environment affects all of us to some degree. We are so consumed with TVs, computers, phones, internet, and the list goes on. Some people have even come to the point where they can't sleep unless there is something helping them: white noise from a fan, the sounds of the ocean, sleeping pills, and any other way to numb the pain of quiet.

How did this happen? Slowly... yes, slowly... but steadily. Technology and a fast pace have increased inch-by-inch. Without us realizing it, we have been "hooked" and are being pulled along faster and faster. We are like a hamster on his hamster wheel: running and spinning, not going anywhere and accomplishing nothing, except getting worn out. And we're dealing with this insanity on a daily basis.

Cars have alarms that sound so frequently now, we don't even pay attention to them to see if there is a possible robbery taking place. Just more of the routine noise we have become desensitized to.

Residents in hospitals and nursing homes are literally plugged in. There is a wire for this and a wire for that. There are so many that people become entangled in them. Alarms and beeps are frequently going off in order to "announce" that something needs to be done. The sounds have become so common that they have lost their ability to let staff know when there is a *real* problem. Put a person who is highly sensitive to sights and sounds, or spiritually sensitive to unseen realms, in these settings, and their responses are going to be intense. Even though they are meant to be helpful, you can understand the dread we feel when having to be admitted into that kind of environment.

When you're as sensitive a person as I am, you daydream of quiet, peaceful, unplugged places. Power outages, though inconvenient and troublesome, can be a haven. Think about it: at home, candles are lit in the darkness, causing tensions to begin to slip away, with the soft lighting. The sounds of routine living quiets down and a peacefulness is allowed to enter in. Before long, people gather together and unite as a family. There is nothing else to do except look around and get to know those who live with you, having the chance to actually converse with one another.

Surprisingly, when the power is restored, a few sighs of disappointment may even be heard. The reason being, we know that it means we will soon be drawn back into our separate corners of the house, plugging into something and ignoring one another once again.

The "mentally challenged" are simply more in-tune than most realize. They feel all the pressures of society more quickly and with more intensity than others. When stressors are amplified, they have been seen covering their ears and rocking back and forth in order to calm themselves because of *the world's* insanity — not theirs.

People on heightened alert, or those with conditions like autism spectrum disorder, can also have the same difficulty, needing to wear special headphones in order to block out the craziness of the extremely bright sights and exceedingly loud noises which are constantly being aimed at us. You have to admit that life is extremely loud and over-stimulating! Why do we insist on trying to get those, who actually know better than us, to join us on *our* crazy hamster-wheel of modern society? Remember though, no matter how fast the hamster runs, he still doesn't get ahead... only worn out.

We have mainstreamed the mentally and physically challenged so they could learn from *us*; when in actuality, it's **them** we should be learning from. Here are some words to reflect on:

CELL-phones (like a prison)

inter-NET (being caught like a fish)

the WEB (being caught by a spider)

{Hmmm... makes you think, doesn't it?}

Technology is not completely bad. It's just that we need to find a healthy balance. In order to hear that still, small voice from the Holy Spirit and bring sanity back into our lives before we burn out, we need to S.T.O.P. = **S**omebody **T**urn **O**n the **P**eace:

Turn on the Quiet

Quiet my mind, Lord, amidst this hurried race,
Bring me peace and serenity,
as I adjust to *Your* pace.

Time is of the essence, but not
as the world sees. Relationships with others,
is the way You aim to please.

Every person that we come across,
was put here just by You. And You always
have a purpose for putting them in view.

Sometimes it's for them, sometimes
it's for us. But finding the truth,
is something we must.

We're all on a path that we take with our feet.
Yet our spirit will yearn, until it's
You that we meet!

"Oh come, let us worship and bow down;
let us kneel before the LORD our Maker.
For He is our God, and we are the people
of His pasture, and the sheep of His hand.

~ *Psalm 95:6-7*

When your emotions are on heightened alert
due to trauma, abuse, or being told over and
over that it's all your fault, you're mentally
unstable, or that you're stupid, it can make you

start to question your own sanity. Walking on eggshells, we start thinking: *Maybe they're right, maybe it is my fault. If only I had done this and not that or said something differently.* To have an objective observer say, "Those are lies. It's not your fault. No one should be treated the way they are treating you," is like having someone throw you a lifeline. Words of affirmation can be a literal life*saver*. But to live under that kind of stress for so many years, it takes hearing those healing words of encouragement and lots of consistent, compassionate support in order to start believing the truth. You can feel off balance and insecure for a very long time.

I really don't like having to reveal the details of the mistreatment I received, but I find it necessary to explain how I perceived what was happening and what things were like for me at that time. I have since forgiven those involved, but that doesn't change my story, and maybe as I do, you'll recognize similarities to your own.

Part of my processing was to write down in my journal some of the reasons why I was leaving my current marriage. I needed to do that so I could remember the truth and not go back to him again. I started by remembering the way he often changed his tune:

> We had been talking about going on
> vacation and he told me to go alone.
> Then he said: "I could use a weekend at the
> beach." Then later that same day he said:
> "I can't take all that time off!! You need to
> go alone!!" He then informed me that he
> didn't know how much vacation time he has.
> He'd boast that he just takes time when he
> wants it, and then he'd turn around and
> snap that he can't just take time off.

There were so many mind games:

> He called, and I let it go to voicemail,
> because yesterday he said he missed me
> and would like to talk to me. Today in his
> message, he told me he has filed his divorce
> papers. Then he strained to sound very
> polite, trying to stay in control, as he said
> he would like to get together for dinner,
> in public, and discuss things so we are in

agreement when we go into court. [People were right, I shouldn't feel sorry for him.]

At the same time, I was also dealing with my first "ex," (my children's father):

He was drunk again, and I thought he was kidding when he said something, so I was kind of joking back, not realizing he was being serious, until he began yelling and swearing at me. Because one of my children was in the other room, I just swallowed the insult. But tears were rolling down my face. Why do so many men in my life treat me like I am dirt? I don't get it. I don't deserve that treatment.

When my grandfather passed away, I wanted to have my child be able to go with me to the funeral. He was their great-grandfather, and he was a *great* grandfather! So, I had a friend listen in on the other line as a witness, and I called their dad (my ex) to make arrangements:

He said, "It's not your weekend to have them."

"I'm sorry that my grandfather was so inconsiderate to not die on *my* weekend!" was my response.

He said, "What? … a 95-year-old senior citizen dies and the whole world is supposed to stop?" Then changing topic, he hit me with, "I hear you're getting rid of the second good man in your life!"

I was stunned to find out that my estranged husband told the father of my kids to watch me because he was concerned about my mental stability. I hadn't seen or spoken to my soon-to-be ex for four months, and therefore he had no basis to say that. And with that lie, my ex pulled out that card again, and said that he, too, was concerned about my mental stability and would not allow me to see my child or take them with me to the funeral. He also said a lot of hurtful and hateful things to me. He then threatened that I wasn't going to be able to see the kids until I was mentally stable, or only under supervised visits by him.

After I had gotten off the phone, my friend

(who had been listening in) was crying. She told me that she never heard anyone degrade someone like he did to me. And there was my "lifeline" of affirmation. It *wasn't* just me. My friend's tears said it all.

With the help of others, I began to just take things one step at a time so I would not become overwhelmed. The first to help me was the Director of my life – Jesus. He was taking care of the details of my life, orchestrating it by putting it on people's hearts to ask me in what ways they could help me.

He also directed me to some wonderfully caring professionals as well. I remember telling my counselor "I keep forgetting to breathe." I knew why it was happening: I was still in fear of how I was going to take care of myself. She asked my psychiatrist to come to her office and write me out a prescription, and she counseled me while we waited. Both were very helpful. They told me that whenever I noticed that I wasn't breathing, I was to consciously slow down, relax, and calm myself. They gave me practical breathing techniques. But sometimes even medication and "techniques" were not enough to balance my SeeSaw.

As I was preparing for this book, I came across some medical records and journals about this time in my life. Now looking back, I have a deeper understanding of why I was having so much trouble breathing. That was only part of my story. I had many stressors happening at the same time:

- My grandmother passed away.

- A few months later, my grandfather passed away. I was very close to them and losing them was very traumatic for me. And even though I know where they will be waiting for me, I was still grieving a great loss in my life.

- Their passing led to family members fighting over my grandparents' estate; I was caught in the middle trying not to take sides, because I loved all of them.

- I was in the process of moving.

- I was in the midst of getting away from my current abusive marriage.

- On top of it all, my children's father, my ex, was causing me so much strife about custody matters.

All the breathing techniques in the world and even wise counsel, couldn't calm the raging emotional whirlwinds and fear that were tossing me right off my SeeSaw. I needed to be with people who could assist me 24/7 and help me not just get back on my SeeSaw again, I needed them to help me find it.

Without going through all the details of my hospitalizations, I will sum them up by saying: the professionals use everything they know how to address the behavior and the physiological aspects of emotional overload, but from this side of things, it can feel very frightening — like they're trying to trap you. Looking back, I can see why it might have been necessary, but it wasn't always handled in the best ways. They were only treating the symptoms instead of looking at what may be *causing* the symptoms. I can also see how the mental healthcare system is seriously lacking a holistic approach, especially the spiritual aspect of wholeness.

In all of my hospitalizations in many different places, there was a common theme that I found: we, the patients, were very creative. Whether it was painting, coloring, writing, or all the other creative ways we express ourselves, it became evident that many of us dealing with instability and uncertainty are sensitive and imaginative individuals.

As brilliant as some people considered the very famous artist, Vincent van Gogh to be, the turmoil within his mind can be seen in many of his paintings. Van Gogh had demons of his own to deal with, and the same is true for us. There is a dark, ominous, cloud looming over our heads: the presence of demonic oppression.

There is a very real battle going on in the spiritual realm that often times causes the erratic behavior and physical symptoms that we see appear in the natural. In the institutional setting, this is not being addressed. Neither is the missing piece of the puzzle, that being: there is absolutely no presence of counselors to help with the myriad of emotional hurt, pain and turmoil which are so prevalent in those surroundings. By talking things out, most people are able to solve a lot of their own issues.

In fact, what just happened to me as I was trying to find the right words to express what I wanted to say, is a good example: I asked my friend if she could help me with "how to say it." She said, "Sure," put down what she was doing and gave me her full attention. I started to read aloud to her the beginning of the sentence I was stuck on, and before I knew it — pop! — the words I had been looking for flowed right out of my mouth. My friend never had to say a thing. Having a listening ear is all I needed. And *that* is the all-important missing piece of the puzzle that just can't be found in the psych units of hospitals.

In order to have a quicker and more complete healing, we all need a chance to have our voice heard, to tell our story, and we need each other to help in that process. Professional counselors are wonderful and I appreciate the years of education and training they have. Yet there's nothing better than a friend who understands because they've paced the same floors, cried identical tears, or hit the same proverbial wall and come out the other side. We all need to have our hope restored now and again.

It doesn't require us having all the answers or even the right words to say. Sometimes all we need to do is show up, sit for a little while, maybe have a cup of tea… and listen. You can't effectively ride the SeeSaw unless someone is on the other end. And being there, gives you each the opportunity to lift one another up.

I Promise You Friend

Have you lost your way and you can
only see down?
Christ is who you need, and He can
always be found.
His arms are wrapped around you,
He will not let you go.

114

I promise you, friend, you can't go too low.

Let Him take over and hold onto Him tight.
You're not alone in this battle — fight!

He's the strongest One who can be found.
He's God's own Son, He's all around,
He's under you now, you can't sink any lower,
So don't turn away and say it's all over.

From the pit of hell to heaven above,
no place can escape Jesus' love.

There's so much goodness Christ has in store,
Answer Him now — He's at your door.
Don't wait for another time to say "yes."
The chance may pass, right now it is best.

You've gotta reach out; don't be ashamed.
There are people to help you;
just call out their name.

It may seem like there's no way to survive.
Get yourself up, don't give into the lie.
I know what I'm talking about; I've been
there before. Believe me, friend,
life holds so much more.

Talk to someone, if even a stranger.
Do it now, before there's real danger.

Even though you feel you're losing your mind,
God made you unique — you're one of a kind.
Just take one step, and then one more.
You'll soon find out that you really can soar.

There are so many ways your life can improve.
Please trust me, friend, I've made the move.

*"For I am convinced that nothing
can ever separate us from God's love.*

*Neither death nor life,
neither angels nor demons,
neither our fears for today
nor our worries about tomorrow —
not even the powers of hell
can separate us from
God's love."*

~ Romans 8:38-39 (NLT)

SWINGING FOR

THE FENCES

CHAPTER 6:
Up the
Downside

I know there was a perfectly good ladder on the slide, but wasn't it more fun getting back to the top by climbing up the slide part, gripping to the sides of it with all your might, while your sneakers fought the slippery surface trying to defy gravity? Once in a while you might tumble back down a little, but you'd keep on trying again and again until you successfully reached the top. It was such an accomplishment that the slide back down was really just a way to get you to the bottom so you could try and do it all over again.

As difficult as writing some of this has been, being able to go back in my journals, back in my memories of some very slippery slopes, feels like quite the accomplishment. I remember, as I went through some of the scariest times, telling God that if I could help someone else get through their struggles and get back on top, it would all be worth it. And now here I am. The Lord has put Luke 9:23-24 in my pathway on numerous occasions:

> *"If anyone desires to come after Me, let him deny himself, and take up his cross daily, and follow Me. For whoever desires to save his life will lose it, but whoever loses his life for My sake will save it."*

For years I had been toying with the idea of writing a book that talks about living with the diagnosis of bipolar but kept shying away from it. Whenever I saw this verse though, I knew what God was saying to me about it. When He said *whoever loses his life for My sake,* I felt He was calling me to lose my life by being bold and addressing the fact that I have been living with the challenge of navigating through what is considered a "mental illness" for a long time — way back to when bipolar was called "manic-depressive disorder."

With all the changes that we have endured these last few years, with covid, violence, and all the unrest, depression and anxiety have become much more common. Yet there is still such a stigma around mental/emotional issues. Many think that "strong" people, especially Christians, shouldn't be dealing with mental health issues. What they don't understand is that the devil is a roaring lion, looking for someone to devour. But that enemy doesn't attack us because we're *weak*; he attacks us because we are *strong*.

My heart aches for those who might be feeling condemned or shamed by society. A diagnosis can feel both embarrassing and be a relief at the same time. If there's a name for it, if it's in a textbook, it means it's not just me. These days I'm in good company. There's so much trauma and fear in our world. I couldn't be quiet anymore. I needed to "die to my pride" about sharing this. I needed to show how God has been with me every step of the way; not condemning me, but teaching, guiding, and rescuing me over and over through all the ups and downs.

Like those mistaken people who think abuse in marriage should be tolerated, so many others need to be educated about healing those who have been traumatized and compassionately ministering to those who have been mentally affected by it. By telling my story of how it has affected my life, and the lives of those around me, I am hoping it will have an impact on someone who is going through a similar situation and that it will bring hope and healing to their minds and souls.

I pray it will not only be beneficial for people experiencing bipolar symptoms, but also for anyone who may find themselves in a deep depression (which is the downside of my SeeSaw and where I tend to gravitate to most of the time). I'm also writing to give friends and loved ones a little better understanding of what the effected person you care about might be experiencing.

In the past, I've struggled with whether I should write about the negative things in my life. Afterall, we are told not to go back, but to go forward. Then someone suggested "not to go back" means: don't go back to *doing* it, but it's okay to *talk* about, especially in order to help others. And I really want to help others…

Okay, so I took a little break before continuing because it's still somewhat difficult to look back at the past traumatic times in my life. So I did what any wise woman would do — I ordered take-out Chinese food and got my General Tsao's Chicken fix. And fittingly, I received a fortune cookie which said: *Cleaning up the past, will always clean up the future.* God speaks in more ways than one — even through a cookie! So here I go: I'm moving forward by climbing backward up the slide and sharing with you a section of my journal I haven't been brave enough to publish until now.

I remember my first experience in the hospital. I was laughing one minute and crying the next. I was diagnosed in 1994 as having manic depression. It has been a long road since then.

I was in and out of hospitals. Last count, I have been hospitalized in six or seven different places over the years; sometimes I was in the same one more than once.

There were times when I was admitted for a couple of weeks. But other times I have been in the hospital for months. Those extended stays led to me losing my apartments and twice being left homeless.

I have also had a procedure called Electrode Convulsive Therapy (ECT). It is a procedure where they actually cause the brain to experience a seizure while the patient is under anesthesia. I always felt like Frankenstein when going through that process. I really hated the procedure and have asked not to have them done again. One of the side effects is massive memory loss. I no longer have the ability to remember things on so many levels. Names are hard, and I ask the same question over again. I think I'm meeting someone for the first time, but they remember me, yet I don't have any recollection of ever meeting them before. This is not only frustrating it is embarrassing as well. I hate when people ask me what I did a couple of days ago or even the day before, because I hardly ever remember. I always need to refer to my calendar.

One *benefit,* is that I can watch a movie not realizing that I had watched it before, and I am able to enjoy it all over again. [I do remember my two favorites though: "It's a Wonderful Life" and "Elf."] There are days I feel like the woman in the Adam Sandler movie "20 First Dates." The woman he dated had a concussion and lost her memory, except for the final day which she remembered; it was her birthday. So her family would celebrate her birthday over and over every day. Until Adam Sandler's character finally figured out a way to help her recover. I've seen that movie more than once, but I can't tell you how he got her to recover, because... I don't remember.

Another side effect, while still in the hospital, is that I have trouble writing the way I usually write. I begin with handwriting that looks like a two-year-old wrote it, and the sentences make no sense at all. Thankfully, it improved. I was an excellent speller and now it can be very difficult to figure out how to spell a word correctly, and that really frustrates me, because I have to pause and try my best to get it right.

I have discovered there are two major instances when this illness worsens: the first is too much stress; the second is when I go into denial and stop taking my medication. The reason I stop is because I feel like I'm all better (I recently read on a psychiatrist's coffee mug: "If you're happy and you know it, take your meds"). So stress and denial tend to get me into the most trouble, especially if I haven't seen anyone for a while who knows me, who can recognize that something's off or that I'm not quite myself. And if I go too long without help, bipolar can manifest into catatonia with me. It can go so far that if left unchecked I go into a coma-like state.

One time, my friend was on vacation out of the country and couldn't get a hold of me. So when she returned, she asked the maintenance man to open my door. They found me alone in my apartment. How long I had been that way (days? weeks?) no one knows, including me. I have a vague memory of knowing I was in my apartment, but I was disconnected from reality and was convinced of things like I was not "allowed" to open my eyes or even have a drink of water. I was very sick and suffering from catatonia and dehydration. Stressors, combined with years of just trying to plow through past trauma, had sent me into that state.

Catatonia is one of the brain's many coping mechanisms. It was a way to "check out" of reality and go into survival mode — a protective state, when my mind was overwhelmed and needed a way of escaping what was going on around me. I would appear to be functioning at that point, but then have absolutely no remembrance of what I had been doing, except for what I call "blips." I can remember hearing my friend's voice and knowing that they would take care of me now. Then I blacked out.

I woke up in the hospital, locked up in a hallway again for what appeared to be another lengthy stay. It is difficult to be around so many other people struggling with similar issues.

None of us are at our best; we are all dealing with being locked up and having to wait for the new medications to take effect that they give us. As much as we were in it together, we were all missing so much of what naturally helps the healing process: fresh air, the beauty of nature, the warmth of sunshine, a listening ear, a quiet safe environment, and our loved ones nearby.

Strangely enough, the need for family is so strong that even though we were all strangers in that ward, we began caring about each other. I remember there being a woman during one of my hospitalizations who was motionless and just lying in her bed. We would see her in the morning when they were taking her to be treated. Slowly, but surely, day by day we saw her coming to life and waking up. Then one glorious day, she walked into the TV room all on her own, without anyone holding her up. We were all so excited that we joined in together and clapped for her, which brought us, as the patients, closer together. We also saw her smile for the first time! We finally had something to celebrate. It really was amazing.

We substituted our need for family, to a degree, with our fellow patients, but nothing could be substituted for the healing effects of nature, sunshine, and fresh air. I had been locked up in that hallway for so long that when my social worker took me outside, I cried when I saw a bird walking around on the sidewalk. Oh, how I missed the birds! One other time, while in the cafeteria, there was a pigeon that landed outside the window. Everyone was so thrilled at the sight that we got out of our seats and ran to the window. It's amazing what gets celebrated depending upon what is happening in our lives at that time.

The other missing and helpful part is having someone there to talk to about what landed us in this locked-up hallway in the first place. We needed someone who would be willing to listen to our story, so that we could not only heal by getting different meds, but also by getting heard and listened to, in order to process everything and be able to heal emotionally as well as spiritually.

It still astonishes me that most hospitals don't

have any counselors on the staff! The nurses are there just to pass out the medications, which take up most of their time. Because of that, the nurses aren't able to use the healing power that God graced them with and most likely, it affects the nurses, too. I doubt they went through all those years of schooling just to hand out pills.

Then came an answer to prayer. I learned that you could ask for visits from the pastor. Such a simple thing, and yet what a difference those visits made. He just sat and mostly listened to me, but he also was helpful with the pertinent questions he asked. I told him I missed music, so he brought me the lyrics from some hymns that I knew, and we sang them together. He left me with a copy of the hymns so I could sing them whenever I wanted to.

God used him to minister to my weary soul. I waited eagerly for his next visit. I had a very vivid dream I wanted to tell him about: *I was walking barefoot on a straight path set before me. It was lined with a carpet of soft, brown pine needles. On either side of the path there was a single row of pinecones lining it. I didn't see them, but I could feel the protective covering of trees over me. I was on holy ground and at total peace. I saw a brook in the distance. It, too, was straight and narrow. Other than the brook, everything was bright white. As I got closer, I noticed a woman crouched down on the other side, with her hand extended out to me. She was encouraging me to come closer. As I did, I noticed that the woman's skirt was flowing with swirls of all different colors — mostly shades of blue, pink, gray and white.* As I was telling the pastor all about this dream, he asked me who I thought the woman was. "My guardian angel," I replied. The pastor just smiled. Then he asked me if the water was deep. "No," I said. "She told me it wasn't. I didn't hear a voice though; it was 'a knowing,' a conveying of thoughts, and that was the only thing she told me. *Then, just as I was about to step onto one of the rocks in the brook...* I woke up."

I guess it wasn't time for me to step in and step across to the other side. God must be getting me ready for what comes next. But I was comforted knowing that whatever is on the other side of all this, is going to be beautiful — beauty for ashes.

To me, the dream also gave me assurance that I would be fine with my next move: trying to find a new place to live (this was one of the times that an extended hospital stay, caused me to lose my apartment). I was scared about the whole situation. God had me on a path where I just had to put my entire trust in Him, letting Him take over and allowing others to help me at this time.

> *"The Lord is my Shepherd; I have everything I need. He lets me rest in green meadows; he leads me beside peaceful streams. He renews my strength ... Even when I walk through the dark valley of death, I will not be afraid, for you are close beside me. Your rod and your staff protect and comfort me."*
>
> ~ Psalm 23:1-4 (LRB)

When I read about the Shepherd's rod and staff, it brings me great comfort as I imagine Him using it to keep danger away from me. And that brings me great peace. As scary as that experience in the hospital was, I made a new friend. The Lord, my Good Shepherd, used a pastor (and "pastor" means: shepherd) to walk alongside me in that valley. That's exactly what I needed. As I spoke to him, I was able to solve some questions on my own. He hardly had to tell me anything; his listening ear was great medicine. Pills can only help *calm* the chaos; they can't *cure*. Only God can truly heal. He knew what I needed most, and He did another 8:28!

At one point during a psych unit stay, even though I was unresponsive at the time, two of my friends were allowed to visit. I heard one of them singing a hymn in my right ear. Later, when I was aware and in the present, I asked her what hymn she had been singing to me; she was totally shocked. She could not believe I could hear her singing: *I love You Lord, and I lift my voice to worship You…* (which is hopefully what I am doing right now: lifting my voice to be heard — a voice I have silenced for so many years). I also asked if her mother had been there on my left side during that visit. And again, I was correct. I had felt her loving presence there even though I was catatonic.

As much as catatonia can offer a way to forget overwhelming circumstances, it can steal away time and good memories as well: One time as I was packing up my belongings to be released from the hospital, I was talking with the nurse who was helping me. I was mentioning that I didn't have a Christmas, that I had missed it, and she said, "You *did* have a Christmas. Your children were with you, and they were very tender with you. They also brought you flowers." This was all news to me. By the time I was dealing with reality again, the flowers had gone by, so there was no evidence of my special time with my children.

But my God is my Redeemer, and He says in Joel 2:25 that He *will give you back what you lost to the swarming locusts*. Whatever has caused you loss, whatever the devil has stolen from you, I believe God's Word is true and He will redeem and reestablish, repair and rebuild. It may feel impossible right now, but with God all things are possible.

Because of the frame of mind I was in at the time, this was a particularly scary ride that

I'm about to describe, seen through extremely frightened eyes. It may sound like it was just my imagination, but I believe the unseen realm is just as real as the one we can see. [Feel free to skip past these next two paragraphs if you're sensitive to spiritually dark things.]

I remember being in an ambulance and all I could see was total black. It was so dark, that there were tiny spots of red, like I imagine it looks like in hell. The EMTs voices were evil-sounding and their laughter felt sinister, like they were glad that they had gotten me and that they had won. At the same time, the ambulance was increasingly going faster and faster, it felt to me like well over 90 mph, and there were no sirens on. I was so scared that we were going to crash.

Once admitted to the hospital, I was catatonic and still unable to talk. *This had to be hell*, I thought. I was hooked up to so many machines and wires that I was all tangled up and couldn't escape. Whenever I did try, alarms would go off and the nurses would come back in and hook me up again, and I'd be back into their captivity.

I don't know how to fully explain how I felt, other than to say that I felt trapped, and it was as if I was partly human and partly machine. It was extremely disturbing. I panicked and was so afraid that I would never escape.

God, You want to heal us from even our memories of times like that. You asked me to let You show me where You were during that frightening ordeal:

I know you were really scared back then. But now, I'd like you to close your eyes for a minute, okay? Just think back to that moment, but this time look for Me there. Can you see where I was?

When I close my eyes and concentrate back to that time, I can feel Your kind and protective arms shielding me as You hug me. You were between me and the wires. You were protecting me from all of it!

Yes, I was right there with you. You can never go too far from Me. I am *always* with you. You cannot get away from My loving presence. I give you My Word.

*"Where can I go from Your Spirit? Or where can I flee from Your presence? If I ascend into heaven, **You are there.** If I make my bed in hell, behold **You are there.** If I take the wings of the morning, and dwell in the uttermost parts of the sea, **even there** Your hand shall lead me, and Your right hand shall hold me. If I say, "Surely the darkness shall fall on me," even the night shall not hide from You, but the night shines as the day. The darkness and the light are both alike to You."*

~ Psalm 139:7-12 [emphasis added]

I remember I kept crying out to You, Lord, in my mind, because I was unable to talk at that point. I prayed to You and reminded You of that promise, and that You said that You'd be with me even in hell. Of course, You didn't need to be reminded — but *I* did. I begged and pleaded that You would get me out of the situation and relieve me from the overpowering fear that I was experiencing. And You did! You never left my side, and You delivered me to safety! You came down and lifted me up out of the miry pit and mud:

"He lifted me out of the pit of despair, out of the mud and the mire. He set my feet on solid ground and steadied me as I walked along. He has given me a new song to sing, a hymn of praise to our God. Many will see what He has done and be amazed. They will put their trust in the LORD." ~ Psalm 40:2-3 (NLT)

God is so faithful that even when we're not fully aware, He listens to our heart's cry. At one point, whether it was chemically induced or just me being spiritually in tune with my surroundings, I remember being taunted and dared by demonic voices that challenged me to fall backwards: *If you really think that Jesus will be there, then fall backwards and see if He will catch you!* I was standing in the hallway at the time and people were all around me. I finally got up the nerve to put my trust in Jesus, and stiff as a board I fell backwards onto the floor. There wasn't a person there to catch me, but I am convinced that Jesus, or maybe an angel, supernaturally from the spiritual realm "caught me," because I didn't get hurt at all. My head had slammed to the floor, and I had no pain or any bruises to show for it. As I stood back up again, I remember feeling joyful — because I knew I had been caught somehow by my Savior!

We may not always be looking for Him to rescue us, we may not even realize He's there, but He is always watching out for us. It can take looking back, to recognize how close He really was. This next part of my story was one of those times. Years after that "hellish" experience, I ended up in the hospital again. This time it was for 49 days. Because of the duration of my stay, I was unable to pay my rent and lost my apartment. Part of the reason why I was hospitalized so long was because the hospital couldn't release me until I had somewhere to go.

Eventually, I was discharged to a homeless shelter, in the middle of a city, where I did not feel very safe. After such an extended amount of time in the hospital, I was really nervous. We were able to sleep overnight at the shelter, but after breakfast we had to leave for the day and not return again, until suppertime. I was blessed that I still had my car, so I was able to go places during the day, like the library or malls, etc., but I was so frightened and ashamed, that I didn't talk to anyone at the shelter.

And I was right there with you all that time. Even though you couldn't feel Me there, I was with you. I sent a volunteer to the shelter, and it was someone you knew, remember?

I couldn't feel You then, but in hindsight, I know that You were right there with me. You didn't just send me *anyone*; it ended up being my favorite teacher who I had in the 6th grade! She and I sat on the couch for hours. I finally found someone who I felt comfortable with. I opened up about my hospital stay and what happened in order for me to be admitted. I was so embarrassed, but she sat there with her arm around me, and just lovingly listened. I was able to begin my healing process. The teacher proved to me that *no words* could have power too! Thank You, Father, for placing her there when I needed someone the most. It was not just a coincidence; it was another one of Your

140

"God-incidences."

After that night, I opened up a little more and began slowly coming out of my shell and trusting the women who were there to help me along on my journey. From the shelter, I moved next door into their boarding house for a while. And from there I was able to move into one of their apartments for women and children. At each place I lived, God was guiding me and taking away all my fears, one by one. Like the fear of being in the middle of a city where crime was high. He actually ended up even giving me His peace that passes all understanding. I was able to walk around the city without being frightened. Thank You for that, God!

There is a song written by Beth and Matt Redman that gives such comfort to me. The lyrics are: *Oh no, You never let go, thru the calm and thru the storm. Oh, Lord, you never let go in every high and every low. Oh, Lord, You never let go, Lord, You never let go of me.* It's amazing how this song echoes my life story. Through the years, I have experienced all the highs and lows of bipolar, and Jesus was with me in every calm and every storm. He's never let go, and I know He never will.

I have a picture of Jesus in my living room. Half of His face is in the light and the other half is in the dark. As I look at it, I am reminded of His promises and I'm filled with hope knowing that my Jesus is in the dark, as well as in the light. And light shines very brightly, because whenever there is even a speck of light, the darkness cannot overcome it! He gives us His Light so we can find our way out — victorious and ready to move on.

Years ago, in my attempt to move forward, I had mustered up all my courage and gone back to a psychiatric ward where I had previously been a patient. But I went as a visitor this time, on my own accord. A nurse who I recognized came and unlocked the door to greet me. She asked who I was there to see. I said, "Anyone who would like to have a visitor." She told me that Michael was in the room down the hall, and he would really like one. So, even though I was totally terrified about what I was doing, and with memories flooding back of being there in my own room, I proceeded down the hall. As far as I knew, no one else had ever done what I was trying to do.

I found Michael seated at one of the dinner tables, alone in the empty dining room. I asked if I could join him. I can't remember what we talked about because it was over ten years ago; all that comes to mind is he did most of the talking. And that is exactly what I was there for — my mission was to be a listening ear. But I do remember what the result was: Michael's spirits were lifted by the time I left him... and so were mine. As I was leaving, he told me that he would see me next time I came in.

My biggest regret was that there wasn't a next time. The fear of being labeled "abnormal" and maybe finding the exit doors locked to me if I went back, overwhelmed me. I listened to the lying thoughts that someone would reprimand me for doing this if they found out about my own psychological history, and they'd deem me "unqualified" to do what I was doing. But how much more qualified and capable could someone be? It felt as if in my attempt to take a step forward, I had somehow taken three steps backwards. I just couldn't overcome the fear and go back into that atmosphere...

…Until now!

It feels like I'm starting another new chapter in my life. I even went out the other day and purchased another ring; this time it has a cross on it, along with little pretend diamonds. Once again, I am at another place where I am looking forward to whatever God has in store for me next. He has prepared me, even by writing this all down for you, to climb back up the slippery slide and be that listening ear to someone who needs to just "talk it out." It's my hope that not only would I be able to do that, but that I could get together a team of "unqualified" people who don't fear the locked doors anymore and would be willing to do the same. I proved that it doesn't necessarily need to be a person with a degree to get effective results. In fact, by having paced those same hallways myself, I'm able to listen and understand with a heart of compassion and empathy, and the results will be healing all around.

"Blessed be the God and Father of our Lord Jesus Christ, the Father of mercies and God of all comfort, who comforts us in all our tribulation, that we may be able to comfort those who are in any trouble, with the comfort with which we ourselves are comforted by God."

~ *2 Corinthians 1:3-4*

CHAPTER 7:
Who Wants
to Play?

I grew up in a tight-knit community. All of the houses were on one-acre lots. There were about 15 of us kids who hung out together and we would play games until the streetlights came on — games like wiffle ball, hopscotch, kick-the-can, and dodgeball. We learned how to play by following the rules. Rules to play by are what make a game "a game." They give us structure and a foundation to play by and to live by. God gives us *His* rules to follow to keep us safe, to get along with each other, and to help us have fun together.

I looked forward to every Sunday because it

meant we were going to go to church, and I'd be able to go to Sunday School. I not only loved learning more about Jesus there, I also looked forward to the weekly snack-time routine of the same special graham crackers that had to be split into the right size, then put on a special napkin. To top it all off, there was the ultimate drink of orange "juice" — the same "juice that the astronauts drank!" I remember it well because ordinarily I didn't like the regular orange juice (with all the pulp in it). But who couldn't resist liking the orange powdered drink of astronauts?

Yet before all of that, we had to play the game of "who can get ready for church without getting into trouble?" Well… none of us could. We were supposed to be getting dressed in our "Sunday best," but we were more interested in the game of fooling around and not paying attention to what needed to be accomplished before we went out the door. What seemed to get me into the most trouble was the finishing touch on my outfit — my black patent leather shoes. [Made to shine like new with a little petroleum jelly. Who knew?] Those shoes were absolutely perfect for tap dancing across the kitchen, but it drove my parents crazy, and it left little black marks on the floor. So "no tap dancing on Sundays" became a rule... that I somehow forgot about each time — I just could *not* help myself.

My dad would go to church looking forward to dozing off during the sermon. My mom would have to give him an elbow to jostle him awake. Then when it was time to socialize around the coffee, we'd all find our way to the "Fellowship Hall." I remember listening to the grown-ups talking to each other as they had their own "church snack-time routine." But what confused me is that it sounded like they were gossiping more than fellowshipping. I wondered *is this what Christians do?* Even at this young age, I felt something was not right about it.

My mom's parents lived up the hill from us and I would escape there as often as I could, in order to get away from the constant yelling and wrestling going on at my house. I adored my grandfather because he gave me my faith — not by what he said, but by what he did, and didn't do. And especially because he always let me be… me! Even when I went missing as a toddler in his house, and he came to look for me because I was too quiet, when he found me in the bathroom with powder everywhere (all over my head, my lap, and the whole room, too), even then, he just let out a big belly laugh as he exclaimed, "What are you doing?!" I proudly announced, "PowDoo! PowDoo!" as I held up the bottle of powder to him. So from that day, and literally until the day he died, he called me his "little PowDoo."

My grandmother made us feel special when we were older as she made us soup for lunch and put it in our own special mugs, each with our name on them. She also let us sit on the high barstools at the counter where the kitchen window was. On the outside of the window was a bird feeder. We would try to be as still as possible, waiting for birds to land and make our day. My grandparents also had an aquarium with so many different kinds of fish.

I will always remember the "electric ones." They were bright silver with a neon-looking red stripe lit on them. Going to my grandparents' home was our own little sanctuary.

My grampa's sanctuary was at the Seventh Day Adventist church where he attended. Their Sabbath day is Saturday. I remember one day saying to him, "That's okay, Grampa, you have Saturdays covered and I have Sundays covered," as far as going to church. If there was a rule my grandfather lived by it would be: Worship God and love your family.

Family meant so much to my grandfather. He would call his five children almost daily to see how they were. While he was on his death bed in the ICU and the last family member came into the room, he just kept repeating: my family, my family. He also was praying out loud asking God to forgive him. Even though I know that he went Home and is waiting for me there when I arrive, I was still so very saddened. Not just because of my loss, but also because his children began fighting over his estate. I thought we had a really close-knit family, so I was very confused and heartbroken that all this was going on. I tried my best not to take sides. I realized we were all grieving in our own different ways. But all the arguing and resentment only made it feel worse. This was my family and I loved them all... just like Grampa did.

I was blessed to have two sets of grandparents growing up. They were all so different, but they passed on to us what they each had to offer. My "Grammy" was a fellow poet. She would write a poem on a napkin, or any other writing tablet she could find. Because when the inspiration hit, she needed to get it written down before she "may forget it." Grammy passed along her talent to my Dad and they both passed along their rhyming ability to me.

We learn so much from those who have gone ahead of us. Without them we wouldn't be who we are. God gave us each other — to learn from and grow up with. I'm so thankful for "family" who stand by me and *with* me, both my relatives and my "adopted families" (like church family, support groups and good friends).

Which brings me to a very special supportive

community called: Celebrate Recovery. To help you understand more about the importance of this team of people, I thought I'd share some of my testimony that I gave at a Celebrate Recovery meeting back in January of 2014:

I am here in this program for many reasons: failure in relationships, co-dependency, enabling, and tonight I am going to speak about my mental health. I am glad I can come here and share my life story, both the trials and the praises. Something I recently read, sounded very wise: *Stories from the past can give us pointers for the present.* I hope this is true, because I have done some really embarrassing things in my past. But because of this C.R. program and yielding to Jesus' guiding hand, I have experienced a lot of growth.

When I first began this program, I was a totally different person. I was filled with a sense of doom and hardly spoke up for myself, and always held my head down. I also would never get up in front of a group and speak. That has all changed now.

There was a time that I didn't attend C.R. for a while. But now, I feel like I have come home again — like the prodigal son in the story[12] Jesus tells, who returns home to his father and is welcomed by him, without any scolding or criticism. You, my C.R. family, have done the same for me.

After explaining about my struggles with bipolar and my hospitalizations, I continued:

It came to the point where one day my very concerned 20-year-old son had to sit me down and tell me that I could not live alone again. It was too dangerous. So, he pleaded that I go to some type of facility. I know that was very difficult for him to do. I agreed to look at the options. I ended up finding an assisted living place. It was beautiful — like a bed and breakfast. It was a very clean and welcoming place.

Then in January of 2013, I had recovered enough and was ready to move into an apartment on my own. But this time I was

---

[12] Luke 15:11-32

going to have access to professional services that would help me. Until all the services were in place though, my C.R. sponsor helped me out tremendously. She held me accountable about taking my medications. After I took them, I would text her and let her know. If she didn't hear from me by 10:00 at night, she would text me. I am so grateful for her caring heart.

Once you walk in the doors to C.R. you are welcome back any time. And one of the reasons I am back here is to pay attention to the early signs that this illness might be acting up again. I haven't needed to go back to the hospital since 2013. I've begun to be more open with some people, that I deal with bipolar. I learned that I don't need to handle it alone. I now have a support team that makes sure I remain healthy. I have a nurse who checks in with me, and also a caseworker. And I have the support from you, my C.R. family. You have helped me to get over many hurdles – spiritually as well as emotionally.

Psalm 37:4 is written on the cover of my checkbook: *"Take delight in the LORD and He will give you your heart's desires"* — which He continually does. In John 10:10, Jesus says: *"I have come that they may have life, and that they may have it more abundantly."* I pray that you have the same. Thank you for listening.

Celebrate Recovery is both a provision from God and a "community" that helps me live life more abundantly. I was able to do a lot of tough work by going through the 12-Step Groups of the program. And I became very close to the women who shared their own stories as well. God created that program through two pastors in California, and it has helped countless people in their Christian walk.

I went through the Steps more than once, and it was helpful in different ways each time I worked through them. The first time through, I prayed to God, asking that He would remove my *obsession* of smoking cigarettes. I was so hooked that while I was smoking one cigarette I was contemplating when I could have my next one. I also think I was the only woman at church who smoked, so it was embarrassing being in the church parking lot with my cigarette in hand. It's hard to believe now that I would actually smoke in the car as I was driving, whether I was alone, or had someone with me.

Going through those 12-Steps for a second time really tested and strengthened me. As I mentioned in an earlier chapter, God sent a friend into my life who was going through the same struggle as me. We were both going through getting a divorce from very unhealthy marriages. God put us together, specifically to support one another. There were many times where we would read a passage in God's Word, and share it, only to discover it was exactly what we needed to hear and it was at the perfect time. We were also surrounded by many "sisters" at Celebrate Recovery who helped us. Even though we weren't all going through the exact same issues, we were still able to help one another along the journey each of us was on.

It was quite a while after that, I went through

the Steps for a third time and was finally able to release my hurts from that failed marriage, and actually came to forgive my ex. With God's help and our cooperation, we can do some pretty amazing things! In case you might be struggling with unforgiveness like I was, I'd like to suggest this prayer that helped me to offer forgiveness and get rid of bitterness:

Lord Jesus,

> *I release my resentment. I am not going to punish them in my head anymore. I'm taking them off my plate and giving them to You, because the battle belongs to You — not me. If I don't forgive, if I hold on to bitterness, it blocks me from receiving YOUR forgiveness. Again, this battle is Yours; it's not my fight. You were there and got me through it. I open myself up to Your healing touch. I am putting my trust in You. I know You have my best interest at heart, and You say to forgive them.*

> *Thank You, Jesus, for making a way. Redeem my memory of it. Please come and heal my damaged emotions. Amen.*

I don't want to necessarily stay exactly in

the middle of the SeeSaw. I still like having emotions that go up and down at a manageable rate, rather than being numb with a flatline of emotions. Yet when you have been stuck riding a SeeSaw at full tilt, and have finally found some balance, it can be hard to recognize a normal range of emotions. It is hard not to fear going backwards and being overwhelmed again. That's what makes family, loyal friends, and trained professionals so important. I am extremely thankful for the support of the team that God has placed around me.

Jesus said: *Here on earth you will have many trials and sorrows. But take heart, because I have overcome the world.*[13] His faithful and loving presence through it all has carried me and made me stronger. The truth of His Holy Bible comforts me like a love letter. His promises have given me a foundation to stand on when everything else is spinning, swinging, or bouncing around me.

---

[13] John 16:33b (NLT)

On the Playground of Life

Up & down and round & round,
going through the day.
Sometimes I'm not sure,
should I do this, or maybe do that?

Trying to explain it all
when I barely understand myself.
I need to be strong if I want to be able
to move on.

Here I am
in the middle of the playground,

balancing my SeeSaw;

Then going down the slide,
hoping to land…
…on my feet.
On to the jungle gym.
Why is it named that anyway?
Makes no sense to me.

Now in the sandbox, I come alive —
playing with the soft, cool sand.

Can I go on the swing yet?
I want to be as free as a bird.
Feelings in my stomach leap,
as I go higher in the sky.

There's today's bully who is always so loud.
He's obnoxious as he tortures
the one who falls down.
Rise again.
I will come back.
Better than before.

Absolutely nothing can separate me
from the Father; God told me in His Word.
Oh, how I love the Words! They minister
to me; I feel wrapped in a warm embrace.

Being on the Playground with Jesus
is the best place to be. Come on, join in.
You'll soon discover He brings
balance to the SeeSaw.

He is the King of the Playground of Life.
He is my big Brother; In Him I do trust;
I know He wants what is best for me.

The sun is going down;
In time I will go Home.
But I won't be there alone;
Friends and family are waiting.
Swinging, riding, playing in the sand…

His Playground never closes
Because it's always bright.
It's His light forever and on into Eternity!

Creativity is so common among us;
spirituality flourishes too.
A change is on the way. Get ready for the ride!
You'll see how work can actually feel like play.

I hope you can see now,
there's another Playground to go onto.

It's the one called New Life…

Not every day at a playground is easy and
fun. Over the years I have found some practical
techniques that have greatly helped me when
I recognize negativity or depression trying to

sneak in. Years ago, it really threw me, and I felt like I was going insane. I would want to "fix it" as soon as I possibly could. When my old SeeSaw was unbalanced, I would question myself and cry out to God, saying: *Why am I feeling this way?! Which of the three is it this time?* 1.) *Is it me, am I weak?* 2.) *Is this the illness?* or 3.) *Is this the devil attacking me?* I had posed those three questions to myself on *many* occasions.

I used to just try to pray it away. But back then, I didn't fully understand that I had the power in Jesus' Name, to demand the devil to go away from me, and that he couldn't torment me anymore. I'm learning how to fight any dark thoughts and old lies which the enemy is trying to get me to believe. God is good and would never talk to me using such condemning thoughts. Satan, on the other hand, is the father of lies and deception, and tries to get me to believe things that are just downright wrong.

But to get to the root of an issue and start the healing process, the spiritual, emotional, and physical sides all need to be addressed.

It takes all three in many instances (prayer, wise counsel, and medication) to overcome the attacks. Getting in touch with my counselor, and making sure that my medications are being taken, are what is usually needed to calm my "up and down emotions." So much of them are just the body's chemical responses to the trauma or chaos I am going through. I have learned there are steps that I can take myself to lessen those occurrences. I recognize the symptoms, and I have tools now to counteract them.

Paying attention to why the symptoms might be happening is always a good place to start: I look at all of my circumstances: Did I get enough sleep? Do I have too much on my plate? Am I lacking sunshine and fresh air? Is there an upcoming holiday or maybe an anniversary of a significant event?

Then I cut myself some slack and allow myself to have a "bitter" day, knowing that tomorrow will be a "better" day. I can honestly say, that each time I have done that, the next day has always been better than the day before.

It's talking to God about life, reading the Bible, and reminding myself of His love, that is the best medicine. Let me tell you about something God had me do recently. First, He had me read a version of Romans 8:35-39 from the New Living Translation:

> "Can anything ever separate us from Christ's love? Does it mean he no longer loves us if we have trouble or calamity, or are persecuted, or hungry, or destitute, or in danger, or threatened with death? … No despite all these things, overwhelming victory is ours through Christ, who loved us. And I am convinced that nothing can ever separate us from His love. Death can't, and life can't. The angels can't and the demons can't. Our fears for today, our worries about tomorrow, and even the powers of hell can't keep God's love away. Whether we are high above the sky or in the deepest ocean, nothing in all creation will ever be able to separate us from the love of God that is revealed in Christ Jesus our Lord."

Then He said to me:

Now read it out loud to Me. It will mean more to you and also have a deeper effect if you speak it out loud. Make it more personal by replacing the word "us" with "me" as you read.

Okay, Lord, if You say so:

"Nothing can ever separate me from Your love. It doesn't mean You no longer love me if I have any trouble... Overwhelming victory is mine, through You, Jesus, who loves me.

I am convinced that nothing can ever separate me from Your love. Life can't or death can't, angels or demons can't, any fears I may have about today or tomorrow — the powers of hell can't even separate me from Your love. Does it mean You no longer love me if I am in trouble?"

Of course not! I am precious to You. I'm Your daughter. Wow, it really does help reading it that way. It makes me feel as if I'm having a conversation together with You. This is Your personal Word to *me* and You always keep Your Word. You're so awesome, my dear Father!

Quoting Scripture is the best weapon against negativity. When we make it our own, it gives us an added boost. There are some passages already in first person, and some we can easily make our personal promise from God. Here is one more verse that really helps me. It's Psalm 91:2-4 (NLT), personalized:

> *This I declare about the Lord: He alone is my refuge, my place of safety; He is my God and I trust Him. For He will rescue me from every trap and protect me from deadly disease. He will cover me with his feathers. He will shelter me with His wings. His faithful promises are my armor and protection.*

We all have those dreary days that come along when we just start feeling a little off. Here are some other "coping mechanisms" I have discovered along the way that can help brighten things up:

- ✓ Combine being in God's company by taking a walk, or any type of exercise you like to do. The longer you do it, the more you will benefit from it.

✓ Focus on something uplifting like a good movie, a book, or show that inspires you. Find something that makes you laugh, something lighthearted or silly. Smile, even if you don't feel like it. It registers in your brain that you're okay and it can actually help you feel lighter in the end.

✓ Spending time with a special pet, or even watching the birds and squirrels out your window, can bring comfort. They help remind you that God loves you more than you love your most favorite pet, and with an unconditional love greater than any animal or person could ever give you.

✓ Sitting by a quiet lake, or watching the sunset, gazing at stars, or watching the clouds change as they move past in the sky (maybe even finding hidden pictures in them), can give you a much-needed change of perspective, and maybe even a sense of hope.

✓ Surprisingly, I've found it very helpful to look for ways to help someone else —

whether by a call or a visit, or maybe taking the time to send someone a greeting card or a special text. What a gift to yourself and others, when you go into someone else's world and allow them into yours.

✓ Setting up a time to get together with someone, gives you something to look forward to. Make plans to have fun. Visit on the phone if you can't get out. Read favorite passages or funny stories to each other. Share fond and silly memories.

✓ On literal "dark and dreary days," sit under a sun lamp. If it's only *emotionally* dreary, then maybe get yourself outside and find some real sunshine. There is always the option of taking a catnap curled up in a sunny spot indoors, too.

✓ Power naps can do a world of good. When I can't nap, sometimes I lie down, but keep my eyes open, and reflect on favorite memories. I call this "eye-opened resting." Then I make sure to get to bed at a decent time, maybe even a little earlier than usual that night.

✓ When I can't fall asleep on my own, I read or do some word-search puzzles until it's too difficult to keep my eyes open.

✓ Seeing a counselor or talking to a trusted friend can bring some needed balance and a different perspective almost every time.

I also like to write down favorite quotes, Scriptures, and ideas that bless me, and I keep them to pull out and look at whenever I need some positive things to help balance out my circumstances. I think this is a good time to share some with you:

> "Two types of voices command your attention today. Negative ones fill your mind with doubt, bitterness, and fear. Positive ones purvey [supply or provide] hope and strength. Which one will you choose to heed?" ~ *Max Lucado*

"If you're open and seeking, God will lead."
~ *SJ Sheperd*

"The earth has music for those who listen."
~ *William Shakespeare*

"A failure is not always a mistake; it may simply be the best one can do under the circumstances. The real mistake is to stop trying." ~ *B.F. Skinner*

"Difficulties don't *determine* who we are. Rather, they *reveal* who we are."
~ *David Jeremiah*

Like with any new game, the first thing we want to know is how to play. Then we usually ask: So, how do you win? If the rules are simple enough, and you think you can win, you will probably jump right in no problem. But when instructions get complicated and really hard to understand, if the game looks too hard, it can be tempting to quit before we even start.

God knows, life is not a game. The challenges we face can make us want to quit altogether.

But He's given us His Word that all of those challenges can be used to help us move forward. He guarantees us that with Him on our team, we will win. It helps to follow the rules, yes, but if we mess up, He'll work it out for us if we ask Him. He'll even pull an 8:28 if need be. So no quitting.

Let's get back in the game… together.

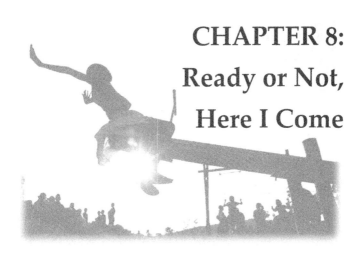

CHAPTER 8:
Ready or Not,
Here I Come

Evidence of Spring

Early this morning, tiny green
buds on the branches.
By dusk, tiny white flowers burst
  open like kernels of white popcorn!

Up ahead the ground was wet,
but I was as dry as could be.
Left behind was the fresh, clean
            scent of the rain gone by.

Although I didn't see these things
take place, the evidence of spring
            had been left all around.

There is a movie about people who had been catatonic and unresponsive, coming back to life again and it's appropriately called *Awakenings*. Robin Williams stars as a doctor in a psychiatric ward who comes up with a treatment which brings patients back to life. It's a must see if you ever want to understand a little better what catatonia is all about.

People have told me that when I have been catatonic, they would lift my arm up in the air and when they let go, my arm would stay right where they put it – like it was frozen in midair. I hate to admit it, but that is exactly how I see some of us "Christians" who live here in New England. The spiritual climate can be as cold as our northern winters and fear of rejection by cold-hearted sceptics have left many of us paralyzed. We have earned the title of *The Frozen Chosen*. Being called "chosen" gives me hope though. Now if we could somehow melt the "frozen" part of our title away.

I love the scene from the movie based on *The Chronicles of Narnia: The Lion, The Witch, and the Wardrobe by C.S. Lewis*, where many of the characters have been frozen by the witch and can only be thawed out by the breath of the Lion (who represents Jesus in the story). The warmth of God's love is the only thing that can melt the cold-hearted. Afraid or not, we are the ones who are called to minister that love to others. It's my prayer that God's love will melt all the frozen hearts and give them all new life.

God, give us the courage to help make that happen.

I know with every fiber of my being, that it *can* happen — nothing is too hard for Him. I believe He wants that for us even more than I yearn for it. God's people around the world are being stirred up. In order for us to awaken fully, we need to remember God's promises. They are better than any ECT treatment. God's "E.C.T." stands for: **E**verything **C**omes **T**rue if it is in the Lord's Handbook (His Bible). It will all happen just as it is written. God spells out everything, and everything He says will come true one day — one glorious day *for those who are the called according to His purpose.*[14] I truly believe that the

---

[14] Romans 8:28

"Frozen Chosen" church-goers hiding in the pews will come back to life again. How? By remembering their first true love — Jesus the Savior — and He will melt their hearts.

I've always known God. On more than one occasion, I have declared that Jesus is my Savior and that I trust Him with my life. I've asked Jesus "into my heart" and told Him I would do whatever He had in mind for me, no matter how challenging (like writing this book). And yet, I have gone through what I call "Salvation Scares," when I wonder if I really have been rescued by Jesus out of the darkness of sin. I've heard some testimonies of people who were alcoholics and then never touched a drink again after believing Jesus is their personal Savior, and it makes me start to question if *I'm* really "saved" because there were never any big, dramatic changes in *my* life like that.

It's been a while since I have had one of these "scare attacks." And that is exactly what they are — attacks from the evil one. He tries to scare me into thinking that I am going to go to hell and not to heaven, by throwing Matthew 7:23

(out of context) at me. In the story, Jesus is talking about the future when He will say to some people pretending to be His followers: *Get away from Me, I never knew you.* The devil lies that God will say that to me when I come face to face with Him someday. I was talking to someone about these enemy scare attacks and he said something I thought so profound: "You must be saved, otherwise you wouldn't care if you were or not." That made so much sense to me. So simple! God doesn't make things difficult, and He always provides a way. And now, I never have to accept that old lie from the devil anymore.

When one lie doesn't work, he'll try to get to me from a different angle. Like when I'm doing something for the Lord, satan will try to distract me by making me feel that I'm going to die soon, and that I won't be able to accomplish the plans the Lord has for me. He tries to get my mind off what I am doing in order to distract me. It's said *if the devil can't destroy you, he'll distract you.* But I have been entangled in that web so many times before, I'm on to him!

Now God helps me to concentrate and use that energy I would have been wasting on being worried, to do what He wants of me. Either I go home to Jesus, or I continue serving the Lord here — either way, I win.

"...being confident of this very thing, that He who has begun a good work in you will complete it until the day of Jesus Christ." ~ Philippians 1:6

My loving Heavenly Father repeatedly puts people around me who help me get away from that kind of "stinking thinking." He sends people who bring comfort and hope with Scripture verses to counteract the enemy's lies.[15] Proof once again, that not only is God right there on my SeeSaw with me, but He often uses others to get on the SeeSaw with me and bring me balance. Whether I need someone right next to me who's on my side, to help me stay level, or a few extra friends sitting across from me to lift me back up, God knows just who they need

---

[15] There's a great online article that addresses this issue: "7 Proofs Your Salvation Is Eternally Secure" blog.biblesforamerica.org/eternal-security-verses/

to be, and when to bring them my way. Here are a few of the verses they have brought to me to raise me up, or calm me down:

"Believe on the Lord Jesus Christ and you will be saved, you and your household."

~ Acts 6:31

"And I give them eternal life and they shall never perish; neither shall anyone snatch them out of My hand. My Father who has given them to Me is greater than all; and no one is able to snatch them out of My Father's hand. I and My Father are one."

~ John 10:28-30

"Have I not commanded you? Be strong and of good courage; do not be afraid, nor be dismayed, for the LORD your God is with you wherever you go." ~ Joshua 1:9

"The unfailing love of the LORD never ends! By His mercies we have been kept from complete destruction. Great is His faithfulness; His mercies begin afresh each day." ~ Lamentations 3:22-23

Be Someone New

God made us for a purpose —
it's true — can't you see?

A purpose for everyone — for you and for me.
Going on a journey to find out what that is.
There's something for everyone,
whether a Mr. or Ms.

We all started out as a seed within our mother.
God made us all special; we should
love one another.

Individuals we are — no fingerprint's
the same. God knew who you were
when He called out your name.

How did He know what your name would be?
He's the Almighty Father of you and of me.

Words are all it takes for the Master
to create. They're really important;
their meaning is great.

So don't throw around words that you'll
regret later on. Our words have much power;
they linger, they're strong.

So while we are here, speak words
that give life. Don't speak the ones
that can cause so much strife.

We all have a day that we can't change
the date. It's the day we were born;
we weren't early, or late.

Our time here on earth is for only one reason.
To love one another, no matter the season.

So if you're wondering what I'm
trying to say: We will all move on;
we will go on our way.

It's up to us, to choose which place it will be.
With Him or without Him — for all eternity.

Now if you're not sure which way you will go,
just call out to Jesus — say yes,
don't say no.

God made something happen when He hung
upon that tree. Why did He do it?

'Cause He loves you, and He loves me.

He died just for you so that you
could be saved. And three days later,
He was raised from that grave!

Together forever, that's how
it should be. Call out to Him now;
get down on your knee.

You want to be joined with those
who you miss; they're waiting at Home
to give you a kiss.

You don't know the hour or even the day.
It could be tomorrow; no one can say.

God wants you to come back
to your Home up above. But you must
confess, that it's Him who you love.

They all want you there
(Father, Spirit, and Son).
You'll be so happy; you'll jump and you'll run.

We need to move on now, there's so
much to do. 'Cause, hurray! It's time
to be someone new!

"Now glory be to God! By His mighty power at work within us He is able to accomplish infinitely more than we would ever dare to ask or hope."

~ *Ephesians 3:20 (LRB)*

Easy as ABC...

"Seek the LORD while He may be found, call upon Him while He is near."

~ *Isaiah 55:6*

We all have one thing in common — a birthday. Our Creator predestined us to have a certain day to be born, and that date can never be changed. We have another thing in common, too: Jesus calls out for us to be born a second time. This time we have the choice over what date that will be.

He also has a special plan for each of our lives. It is predestined for us. All we have to do is answer His call and receive His Holy Spirit. We all have a specific purpose in this life. God created us that way, and He wants us to go on the journey of discovering what exactly that calling is.

"For by Him all things were created that are in heaven and that are on earth, visible and invisible... All things were created through Him and for Him." ~ Colossians 1:16

Not only were we created **through** God, but we were also created *for* God. We are not here to sit around all day playing video games. We have Kingdom work to do here, in preparation for the day we go Home to Jesus. Because of this verse I had been asking God continually, "What am I here for? What do You want me to do? I need to know what my purpose is. I want to know so that I can start doing it!"

We will not know what our calling is until we answer yes to Jesus. He is continually calling out, inviting us to be a part of His family. If we choose not to, we will lose out on living the abundant life that we were predestined for here and now, and we'll miss spending eternity with Him in Heaven. We just need to trust Him.

There has never been anyone more in love with you, than Jesus is right now. Saying yes to His invitation to step out of darkness and insecurity, into the light of His Kingdom and blessed assurance, is as easy as A.B.C.

ADMIT we have sinned (we all do):

"If we say we have no sin, we are only fooling ourselves and refusing to accept the truth. But if we confess our sins to Him, He is faithful and just to forgive us and to cleanse us from every wrong." ~ *1 John 1:8-9 (LRB)*

BELIEVE that Jesus died on the cross to pay the penalty for *our* sins, not His sins, because He was perfect. He was the spotless Lamb of God, sacrificially given up for us.

"For God decided to save us through our Lord Jesus Christ, not to pour out His anger on us. He died for us so that we can live with Him forever..." ~ *1 Thessalonians 5:9-10*

COMMIT our life to Him and serve Him here by loving and serving one another. King Jesus' commission to all of us is to share the Father's love and be His representatives here on earth. We're to go into all the world and love people in order to bring them into His Kingdom.

"But you are a chosen generation, a royal priesthood, a holy nation, His own special people, that you may proclaim the praises of Him who called you out of darkness into His marvelous light..." ~ 1 Peter 2:8-10

If you would like to make Jesus the Lord of your life, you can say this prayer, or use your own words:

Dear Jesus, I come before You today to tell You that I am truly sorry for all the times I have sinned against You. Thank You so much for dying on the Cross for me, which paid the penalty for all my sins. I want to be able to hear You better and understand Your Word, so I'm asking You to empower me with Your Holy Spirit so that I may serve You. Thank You, Jesus. Amen

When you accept Jesus into your life you can begin going on a journey of discovering what God's will is for your life. It's an exciting process! I recommend that your next step is to get your hands on a Bible and dig in. Then tell someone who can help you find a group of followers of Jesus Christ. It's important to be with other Christ followers, especially so you can study His Word together; then be amazed as you hear from God in a new and exciting way. You'll soon discover:

There's JOY in the JOurneY.

"… as our confidence in the Father grows, we'll find ourselves depending on Him more. Then difficulties won't shake us as easily because His peace and joy will guard our heart and our mind." ~ *Charles Stanley*

Don't let the enemy keep you down with condemnation about your past experiences. Learn from them and share them but move on into your destiny – the destiny the Lord had laid out before you. *We don't **decide**, we **discover** God's plan for us.*[16] Before you were even born, He had your future already planned out for you. He knew what you would have to endure and how you would come out of it victoriously instead of remaining a victim.

Anne Ortlund once said that *whatever God asks*

---

[16] *Jentezen Franklin*

187

you to be, He enables you to be. The Lord has been showing me how true that all is.

> **Enjoy My peace amidst your suffering, which will in turn, bring everlasting healing. Remember, you did not choose Me, but I chose you... and I've promised to supply you with all that you need according to My riches in glory by Christ Jesus. [17] Are you ready? Let's get to work...**

You'll see how work
can actually feel like play.
I hope you can see now,
there's another Playground to go onto.
It's the one called New Life...

It's time we look around
and see with brand new eyes.
We're really not alone.
Our voices will now be heard.
A change is on the way...

... Get ready for the ride!

---

[17] John 15:16, Philippians 4:19,

More From the Author:

If you have enjoyed this book, you may want to read Sue's first book:

This is Why I Sing
…and you can too!

Do miracles still happen? You bet they do! In this book you will read about more than one. You will discover just how powerful words are and how God's Holy Spirit can be revealed through poems. Did you know that God is actually singing over you? It's true! Jesus wants to know you more intimately and He is closer than you can imagine. Come learn the many different ways that He is reaching out to you. And learn how and why you can sing back to Him.

Available on Amazon.com

About the Author:

The author chose "Just Sue" as her pen name, because throughout her many years of writing, she has had several different last names. She has now grown to realize that just "Sue" is enough. Although she has authored numerous inspirational poems and published several of them prior to writing her first book, publishing this, her second book, has been her dream for many years. She has used her poems in the past to share her heart, but now she's found her voice in storytelling as well.

Sue, who's a life-long New Englander, has been blessed with three adult children, two daughters-in-law and two grandchildren (and we can't forget the five grand-dogs). You are welcome to contact the author at her email:

JustSue4@gmail.com

****

Suggested resource: CelebrateRecovery.com

Made in the USA
Middletown, DE
25 October 2023

41367843R00116